Information Processing with COBOL

Terry Marris

Lecturer in Computing,
Charles Keene College of Further Education

Edward Arnold

A division of Hodder & Stoughton
LONDON   NEW YORK   MELBOURNE   AUCKLAND

© 1989 T. Marris

First published in Great Britain 1989
Distributed by Routledge, Chapman and Hall Inc.

British Library Cataloguing Publication Data
29 West 35ᵐ Street, New York, NY 1001.

British Library Cataloguing in Publication Data

Marris, Terry
  Information processing with Cobol.
  1. Computer systems. Programming languages:
  Cobol languages
  I. Title
  005.13′3

ISBN 0–7131–3636–7

Typeset in 10/11pt Times by TecSet Ltd, Wallington, Surrey.

Printed and bound in Great Britain for Edward Arnold, the edu-
cational, academic and medical publishing division of Hodder and
Stoughton Limited, 41 Bedford Square, London WC1B 3DQ by
J. W. Arrowsmiths Ltd, Bristol.

Preface

READERSHIP

This book is intended for any student who needs to complete a programming project, or who needs to answer examination questions on information processing systems, or would like examples and explanations of COBOL programs. Students following courses such as the City and Guilds 418 Computer Programming and Information Processing, GCE A-level in Computing Science, BTEC Diploma in Computer Studies, HNC or HND in Computer Science will find this book useful.

SCOPE

This is a practical book. It shows how to design programs for common data processing tasks and how to analyse and design simple business information processing systems. The descriptions of information processing systems provide the context in which the computer programs are used.

The early chapters contain many small examples and exercises to help the beginner gain confidence and develop skills in problem solving. Program design is taught by using stepwise refinement, structured English and dry-runs. Attention is paid to choosing test data. Top-down design and modular programming are used in later chapters to show how to design and write large programs.

Towards the end of the book, the descriptions of information processing systems provide suggestions for project work. This book shows how to analyse and design systems by using data flow diagrams and system flowcharts.

The programming language used is COBOL. This book is not intended as a beginner's comprehensive textbook on COBOL, although a considerable amount of COBOL syntax is introduced; rather, it is intended as a beginner's guide to programming for business information processing systems.

COBOL is available for most microcomputers. COBOL dialects differ from one another mainly in the statements used to control output to the screen. The examples of screen formatting programs are written in Microsoft COBOL. Programs written in MicroFocus COBOL can be found in the appendix. Whatever version of COBOL is used, this book will help make COBOL comprehensible.

ACKNOWLEDGEMENTS

My chief thanks must go to Sheila Catton who made a considerable contribution to this book. She freely gave her time to discussing its nature and content and I have adopted many of her ideas. By painstakingly reading successive drafts she pointed out ways in which the style could be improved and instances where errors occurred. Nevertheless, any shortcomings which remain are entirely my responsibility.

Many other people, colleagues and students, contributed directly or indirectly to this book; to them I give my thanks.

The NCC Display Charts are used by permission of the National Computing Centre Limited, Manchester.

The City and Guilds of London Institute examination questions are reproduced by their permission. The worked examples and answers are not in any way authorized by, or the responsibility of, the Institute.

CP/M is a trademark of Digital Research.

Terry Marris

Contents

1
Introduction

1.1 ALGORITHMS

How would you boil an egg? Most of us have followed a sequence of steps to accomplish some task, or given instructions for someone else to follow. A sequence of instructions is called an algorithm. Examples of algorithms are:

> instructions for boiling an egg;
> a method for making bread;
> a knitting pattern for a pair of socks;
> instructions for constructing a model aeroplane;
> rules for finding a book in a library;
> instructions to a computer.

The purpose of this chapter is to show how we can begin to write a sequence of instructions which can be carried out by a computer.

We start by looking at the steps involved in finding the sum of a list of numbers. Suppose our list comprises 3, 9, 7, 2 and 8. We might proceed thus.

step 1: read the first two numbers in the list, add them together and call the result sum-so-far: 3 + 9 = 12, sum-so-far = 12
step 2: take the next number in the list, add it to sum-so-far and call the result sum-so-far: 7 + 12 = 19, sum-so-far = 19
step 3: repeat step 2 until there are no more numbers to be added to sum-so-far:
2 + 19 = 21, sum-so-far = 21
8 + 21 = 29, sum-so-far = 29
step 4: declare that the sum of the numbers in the list is the final value of sum-so-far:
'The sum of the numbers in the list is 29'

Would this algorithm produce the right results for a list of any length? If our list contained just one number, say 7, then we could not carry out step 1 because we could not read the first two numbers. Although we could read the first number, we could not read the second because it does not exist. Suppose we start off by asserting that sum-so-far = Ø. Then we might write

step 1: give sum-so-far the value 0

step 2: read the next number in the list, add it to sum-so-far and call the result sum-so-far
7 + 0 = 7, sum-so-far = 7

comment

when no previous numbers have been read, the next number is the first in the list

step 3: if there are more numbers to be added, then repeat step 2

there are no more numbers so we proceed to step 4

step 4: declare that the sum of the numbers in the list is the final value of sum-so-far
'The sum of the numbers in the list is 7'

All this effort for just a simple addition! We have used English to design the algorithm. Although English is an excellent and natural problem solving tool, we need to design and write our algorithms in such a way that our design can easily be translated into a programming language. We can achieve this by using what is called *structured English*.

1.2 STRUCTURED ENGLISH

The rules of structured English are few and simple.

1 Keywords like *if, then, repeat, while, do* are used
2 The 'sentences' are set out in a meaningful and helpful manner

1.2.1 IF . . . THEN . . . OTHERWISE . . . ENDIF

The following example illustrates the use of the keywords *if, then* and *otherwise*.

```
if (exam-mark is less than 40) then
    write "fail"
otherwise {exam-mark is 40 or more}
        write "pass"
endif
```

Although we have underlined the keywords in this example, we do not usually do so when writing structured English. The strange word endif merely marks the end of the if . . . sentence.

If the value of exam-mark is 39, say, then the condition (namely exam-mark is less than 40) is met and the 'fail' message is written.

If the value of exam-mark is 41, say, then the condition (exam-mark is less than 40) is not met and the 'pass' message is written.

Either one message, or the other is written.

Words of explanation, inside curly brackets, are used wherever they help make the meaning clear to the reader.

Notice that, in the above example, the commands 'write "fail"' and 'write "pass"' are *indented*. This helps to clarify which command is to be carried out if the condition exam-mark is less than 40 is satisfied and which command is to be carried out if the condition is not satisfied.

Instructions or commands are often called *statements*. If an instruction is carried out, we say it is *executed*.

1.2.2 REPEAT N TIMES . . . ENDREPEAT

Where instructions are to be repeated a known number of times, the keywords *repeat* and *times* are used. For example, if a mark list contained the names and exam marks of 25 candidates, we might write

```
repeat 25 times
        read next name and mark
        write name
        if (mark < 40) then
            write "fail"
        otherwise
            write "pass"
        endif
        endrepeat
```

Again, the keywords are underlined. The strange word endrepeat merely marks the end of the instructions to be repeated. The set or block of instructions to be repeated are enclosed between repeat 25 times and endrepeat. Further, the block is indented. This algorithm means:

for each of the 25 candidates on the mark list
    write the name and whether the candidate has passed or failed.

1.2.3 WHILE ... DO ... ENDWHILE

The keywords *while* and *do* are used where a sequence of instructions is to be repeated, but we do not know precisely how many times. For example:

From a list of exam candidates and their marks, find the average mark.

The instructions to be repeated for each candidate are:

    read the next candidate's mark
    add mark to sum-of-marks
    add 1 to number-of-candidates

But we do not know how many candidates there are. So we write

    while (not at end of list) do
        read next mark
        add mark to sum-of-marks
        add 1 to number-of-candidates
    endwhile
    calculate average
    stop

The term endwhile explicitly marks the end of the group of statements to be repeated. Notice that these statements are indented. The algorithm means

1   check for the end of the list:
        if the end of the list has not been reached, then
            go to step 2
        if the end of the list has been reached, then
            go to step 6
2   read the next mark
3   add mark to sum-of-marks
4   add 1 to number-of-candidates
5   go to step 1
6   calculate average

Step 1 corresponds to while (not at end of list) do and step 5 corresponds to endwhile. In other words, as long as (i.e. while) the condition (not at end of list) is met, keep on reading marks and adding.

Before we can add the first candidate's mark to sum-of-marks, sum-of-marks must have a value, namely zero. We write

    sum-of-marks ← 0

to mean give sum-of-marks the value zero. The arrow, ←, means *becomes*. So, we can say sum-of-marks becomes zero. A similar argument applies to number-of-candidates.

```
sum-of-marks ← 0
number-of-candidates ← 0
while (not at end of list) do
        read next mark
        add mark to sum-of-marks
        add 1 to number-of-candidates
endwhile
calculate average
```

When we have added the last candidate's mark to sum-of-marks, we need to calculate and write out the average mark. The average mark would be calculated from

$$\text{average-mark} \leftarrow \frac{\text{sum-of-marks}}{\text{number-of-candidates}}$$

provided number-of-candidates was not equal to zero (division by zero is not defined by our usual rules of arithmetic). This could be possible, for example, if a class had entered for several subjects, but no one had entered for a particular subject.

```
if (number-of-candidates = 0) then
        write "no candidates in list"
otherwise {number-of-candidates not = 0}

        average ←      sum-of-marks
                    number-of-candidates

write average
endif
stop
```

Our completed algorithm to find the average mark from a list of exam marks is

```
sum-of-marks ← 0
number-of-candidates ← 0
while (not at end of list) do
        read next mark
        add mark to sum-of-marks
        add 1 to number-of-candidates
endwhile
if (number-of-candidates = 0) then
        write "no candidates in list"
otherwise {number-of-candidates not = 0}

        average ←      sum-of-marks
                    number-of-candidates

write average
endif
```

sum-of-marks and number-of-candidates are examples of *variables* because their values change during the execution of the algorithm. But what about average? It has one value only assigned to it, namely, the result of dividing the final value of sum-of-marks by the final value of number-of-candidates. However, the value of average will usually not be the same every time the algorithm is executed because its value depends upon which particular list of candidates is being processed. Therefore, average is also an example of a variable.

Notice that the names we gave to our variables are *descriptive*. For example, the purpose and meaning of the variable named average is easily understood by anybody who has to read the algorithm. To help people understand our algorithms, we avoid using variable names like 'a' because the meaning of such a variable name is not immediately clear. Further, we avoid including spaces in our variable names. For example, instead of writing sum so far, we write sum-so-far because sum-so-far represents a single variable: sum so far could be confused for three variables.

The names which we use to describe variables are often called *data names* or *identifiers*. A particular value of a data name is often called a *data value* or a *data object*. A *data item* is a data name together with its data value.

Example 1.1

Write and test an algorithm which will find and state the lowest number in a list of five numbers.

A possible answer is

```
find-lowest {this is a descriptive name for the algorithm}
    read next number
    lowest-so-far ← number
    {The first number read is the lowest number so far.}
    {There are now 4 numbers to be read left in the list.}
    repeat 4 times
        read next number
        if (number < lowest-so-far) then
            lowest-so-far ← number
        endif
        {If the number read is less than the lowest number so far,}
        {then the number just read becomes the lowest so far.}
    endrepeat
    write out lowest-so-far
    stop
```

Notice the absence of an 'otherwise' part in the if . . . sentence. No matter whether number is less than lowest-so-far or not, the statement following the endif (in this case, endrepeat) is executed. There are more elegant solutions — but this one will do for now.

How can we test this algorithm? We could choose a list of five numbers and write down the results of executing the algorithm. Suppose we chose the following numbers for our test list:

$$6, 3, 1, 7, 9$$

We would expect our algorithm to produce the result that 1 is the lowest number in this list. We execute the algorithm step by step to see whether we actually obtain the expected result.

	Variable number	Condition number < lowest-so-far	Variable lowest-so-far	Times
read next number	6			
lowest-so-far ← number			6	
repeat 4 times				
read next number	3	3 < 6? yes	3	1
if number < lowest	1	1 < 3? yes	1	2
lowest ← number	7	7 < 1? no		3
endif	9	9 < 1? no		4
endrepeat				
write out lowest-so-far				
stop				

The first number in the list is read. It is 6. This value is assigned to lowest-so-far.

The next number from the list is read. It is 3. 3 is less than 6, so the value of lowest-so-far becomes 3. We have executed the instructions to be repeated once.

The next number from the list is read. It is 1. 1 is less than 3, so the value of lowest-so-far becomes 1. We have executed the instructions to be repeated twice.

The next number from the list is read. It is 7. 7 is not less than 1, so the value of lowest-so-far remains unchanged. We have executed the instructions to be repeated three times.

The next number from the list is read. It is 9. 9 is not less than 1, so the value of lowest-so-far is unchanged. We have executed the instructions to be repeated four times.

The instructions to be repeated have been executed the required number (i.e. four) times, so we proceed to the next statement, which instructs us to write out the latest value of lowest-so-far. This value is 1, which is the expected result.

If the actual result had not matched the expected result, then a mistake in the design of our algorithm might have been made (in which case we would need to re-design it) or we might have made a mistake in executing it.

Notice that our choice of numbers in the test list has caused us to execute every statement in the algorithm at least once. Notice also how the results of executing our algorithm are recorded. For each data name (e.g. number) and condition (i.e. number < lowest-so-far?) that occurred in the algorithm, there is a column. As we step through the algorithm, the values of the data names and the results of testing the condition are recorded in the appropriate columns. This is an example of a *dry run* or a *walkthrough*.

Exercise 1.1

1   Design (in structured English) and test an algorithm which will find the highest number in a list of six numbers.

2   Design an algorithm which will produce the message 'in credit' or the message 'overdrawn' or the message 'empty' depending on the amount of money in a bank account, allowing for whole numbers of pounds only. Test your algorithm three times: once with −1, once with 0 and once with 1 as three distinct values of an amount of money in a bank account.

3   Design an algorithm which will produce the number of dollars corresponding to an amount in pounds sterling if there are 1.50 dollars to the pound. Use simple numbers when testing your algorithm.

4   Design and write an algorithm which will count and display the number of names in a list of names. The last item in the list is to be '***' and it is not to be included in the count. Test your algorithm with lists containing zero, one and three names respectively. (A list with zero names will have one item, namely ***.)

5   Design and write an algorithm which will produce a list of names and results (pass, credit or distinction) from a list of names and exam marks when the minimum mark for a pass is 40, for a credit is 58 and for a distinction is 75. The exam marks all lie within the range 0 to 100 inclusive. To test your algorithm, use marks with values of:

    39, 40, 41 {boundary between fail and pass}
    57, 58, 59 {boundary between pass and credit}
    74, 75, 76 {boundary between credit and distinction}

2

COBOL from Structured English

2.1 COBOL PROGRAMS

In this chapter we see how COBOL programs are written. First, we examine the main features of a simple COBOL program, then we see how to translate structured English algorithms into COBOL.

Here is a program to display the word 'help' on the screen.

```
IDENTIFICATION DIVISION.
PROGRAM-ID. TM21.
ENVIRONMENT DIVISION.
DATA DIVISION.
PROCEDURE DIVISION.
PARAGRAPH-1.
    DISPLAY "help"
    STOP RUN.
```

Throughout this book, COBOL programs are presented in upper case. This enables us to easily distinguish COBOL from the text of the book.

In Every Darned Program there are four DIVISION headings, namely:

IDENTIFICATION DIVISION.
ENVIRONMENT DIVISION.
DATA DIVISION.
PROCEDURE DIVISION.

and they occur in this order.

The IDENTIFICATION DIVISION contains a PROGRAM-IDentifier. For this example I have chosen the name TM21 to identify the first program in Chapter two written by Terry Marris. You should choose your own program names.

The purpose of the ENVIRONMENT DIVISION and of the DATA DIVISION will be explained later.

The PROCEDURE DIVISION contains the algorithm. The algorithm in this example is:

```
DISPLAY "help"
STOP RUN.
```

This DIVISION is organised into paragraphs. In this example, there is only one paragraph which we have chosen to call PARAGRAPH-1.

Imagine that the paper on which you write your COBOL is organised into columns and that each column has the width of one character. Paragraph names and DIVISION headings begin in column eight. Statements comprising the algorithm usually begin in column twelve. Statements do not begin to the left of column twelve, nor do they extend beyond column 72. The same rules apply when you enter a COBOL program into the computer.

column 8

```
IDENTIFICATION DIVISION.
PROGRAM-ID. TM21.
ENVIRONMENT DIVISION.
DATA DIVISION.
PROCEDURE DIVISION.
PARAGRAPH-1.
    DISPLAY "help"
    STOP RUN.
```

column 12

Notice the full stops: their presence (or absence) is important. They occur after every DIVISION heading and paragraph name and at the end of each paragraph. They also occur elsewhere — as we shall see.

A program contains instructions to a computer. Each instruction could cause a computer to carry out some task like making a calculation, displaying a message or making a selection between alternatives. When a computer carries out an instruction we speak of the instruction as being *executed*. In a sense, each instruction is a command to a computer, and therefore has some measure of *control* over what a computer does.

Exercise 2.1

Test the program which displays the word 'help' on your computer. You will have to use a text editor or word processor to create the program text on your computer, a COBOL compiler to translate it into code and then a link-loader to complete the translation into a form the computer can execute. If necessary, ask an expert for help with editing, compiling and executing your program.

2.2 SELECTIONS

In the last chapter we examined the meaning of the algorithm

```
if (exam-mark is less than 40) then
    write "fail"
otherwise { exam-mark is 40 or more }
    write "pass"
endif
```

This structured English algorithm translates naturally into COBOL.

```
      IF (EXAM-MARK LESS THAN 40)
          DISPLAY "fail"
      ELSE
*         { exam-mark is 40 or more }
          DISPLAY "pass".
```

Notice that in COBOL 'then' is not used. Notice also that the structured English otherwise becomes ELSE, and that endif translates into a full stop. In COBOL, the full stop is used to mark the end of the IF . . . ELSE . . . sentence. Instead of the words LESS THAN, the symbol < can be used, both in structured English and in COBOL. We have assumed that the words 'pass' or 'fail' are written out on the screen. So, in this instance, the structured English write becomes DISPLAY in COBOL.

A comment in COBOL is written on a line of its own. Such lines begin with an asterisk (*) in column seven. COBOL statements which appear in a comment line are treated as comment and are not executable. The use of curly brackets ({ and }) to mark the beginning and end of a comment are optional. But we include them because if a comment includes words that just happen to be COBOL, then the reader is less likely to be confused by them.

Before the statement

```
if (exam-mark < 40) then
    write "fail"
otherwise
    write "pass"
endif
```

can be carried out, the variable exam-mark must have a value. We require that a value for exam-mark be read. In structured English we might write

```
read exam-mark
```

In COBOL we would write

```
DISPLAY "Please enter an exam mark"
ACCEPT EXAM-MARK
```

This DISPLAY statement, when executed by the computer, prompts the program user to type in an exam mark followed by a carriage return. The ACCEPT statement forces the computer to wait until somebody types in a number and presses the return or enter key. This numerical data value is then assigned to the variable EXAM-MARK.

The structured English algorithm we are going to implement in COBOL is

```
read exam-mark
if (exam-mark < 40) then
    write "fail"
otherwise { exam-mark is 40 or more }
    write "pass"
endif
stop
```

In COBOL:

```
PROCEDURE DIVISION.
PARAGRAPH-1.
    DISPLAY "Please enter an exam mark"
    ACCEPT EXAM-MARK
    IF (EXAM-MARK < 40)
        DISPLAY "fail"
    ELSE
*       ( exam-mark is 40 or more )
        DISPLAY "pass".
    STOP RUN.
```

Now, in COBOL, every data name that appears in the PROCEDURE DIVISION (in our example, the data name is EXAM-MARK) is *defined*. These definitions or *declarations* are written in the WORKING-STORAGE SECTION of the DATA DIVISION.

```
DATA DIVISION.
WORKING-STORAGE SECTION.
01  EXAM-MARK  PICTURE 999.
```

One important point about data names is that they must not be identical to any word which has a special meaning in COBOL. We have already met some of these words: DATA, DIVISION, ACCEPT, for example. To prevent us from inadvertently using a reserved COBOL word as a data name, we shall prefix all data names with **W** (for **WORKING-STORAGE**). For example:

```
W-EXAM-MARK
```

Further, in COBOL, data names should not contain spaces. For example, W EXAM MARK would represent three data items, not one as intended.

We now turn our attention to the line

```
01  W-EXAM-MARK PICTURE 999.
```

The PICTURE 999 clause specifies that W-EXAM-MARK is numeric in nature, that arithmetic can be performed on its data values, and that the value of W-EXAM-MARK is a positive whole number with 3 digits — one digit for each occurrence of a 9 in the PICTURE clause. For example, if a user entered the number 7, then W-EXAM-MARK would contain 007. The significance of the '01' will be explained later.

In future, we shall use the COBOL abbreviation PIC for PICTURE in the definitions of data names.

The complete COBOL program is

```
    *   { This program displays either 'pass' or 'fail' }
        IDENTIFICATION DIVISION.
        PROGRAM-ID. TM22.

        ENVIRONMENT DIVISION.

        DATA DIVISION.
        WORKING-STORAGE SECTION.
        01  W-EXAM-MARK  PIC 999.

        PROCEDURE DIVISION.
        PARAGRAPH-1.
            DISPLAY "Please enter an exam mark"
            ACCEPT W-EXAM-MARK
            IF (W-EXAM-MARK < 40)
                DISPLAY "fail"
            ELSE
    *           { exam-mark is 40 or more }
                DISPLAY "pass".
        STOP RUN.
```

Exercise 2.2

1   Type in, compile and test program TM22. A suitable set of exam marks to test this program would be 39, 40 and 41 because 40 is the *critical point*, i.e. the *boundary* between pass and fail, 39 is *just below* this point and 41 is *just above* it.

2   Produce a tested COBOL program from the following structured English algorithm.

```
        read money-in-bank-account
        if (money-in-bank-account < 0) then
            write "overdrawn"
        endif
        if (money-in-bank-account = 0) then
            write "account empty"
        endif
        if (money-in-bank-account > 0) then
            write "in credit"
        endif
        stop
```

Note:
(a) The otherwise part of the if . . . sentences are not used in this algorithm. Therefore in COBOL we write

```
        IF (W-MONEY-IN-BANK-ACCOUNT < 0)
            DISPLAY "overdrawn".
```

Notice the full stop.
(b) You will need to declare that the variable money-in-bank-account could have a negative value e.g. -23 (pounds) if overdrawn. An appropriate WORKING-STORAGE SECTION entry might be:

```
        01  W-MONEY-IN-BANK-ACCOUNT  PIC S9999.
```

The 'S' specifies a sign (e.g. a minus sign) and permits the variable to have a negative value, e.g. -23. The clause PIC S9999 means that the variable contains four digits. In reality we would allow for more than four digits, and we would cater for decimal values like 15.65 for example. For the moment, we shall ignore these considerations.
(c) Remember to test your program with data values which are close to the critical points.
(d) Use just one paragraph in your PROCEDURE DIVISION.

2.3 REPETITIONS

2.3.1 REPEAT n TIMES . . . ENDREPEAT

This algorithm accumulates the value of goods sold for each day to produce the total for the week.

```
weekly-total ← 0
repeat 5 times
        read next daily-total
        add daily-total to weekly-total
endrepeat
write weekly-total
stop
```

One way of writing this algorithm in COBOL is

```
PROCEDURE DIVISION.
LOOP-CONTROL.
        MOVE 0 TO W-WEEKLY-TOTAL
        PERFORM LOOP 5 TIMES
        GO TO NEXT-BIT.

LOOP.
        DISPLAY "Next daily total"
        ACCEPT W-DAILY-TOTAL
        ADD W-DAILY-TOTAL TO W-WEEKLY-TOTAL.

NEXT-BIT.
        DISPLAY "Total for the week is : " W-WEEKLY-TOTAL
        STOP RUN.
```

The structured English

```
weekly-total ← 0
```

becomes

```
MOVE 0 TO W-WEEKLY-TOTAL
```

in COBOL. This gives the variable W-WEEKLY-TOTAL the value 0.

The structured English

```
repeat 5 times
        read next daily-total
        add daily-total to weekly-total
endrepeat
```

translates into the COBOL

```
PERFORM LOOP 5 TIMES
GO TO NEXT-BIT.

LOOP.
    DISPLAY "Next daily total"
    ACCEPT W-DAILY-TOTAL
    ADD W-DAILY-TOTAL TO W-WEEKLY-TOTAL.

NEXT-BIT.
```

The structured English repeat 5 times becomes PERFORM (a named paragraph) 5 TIMES. The statements to be repeated by executed are contained in the named paragraph.

In this instance, the named paragraph is LOOP. (We use the word LOOP to mean a set of instructions to be repeated). But the name of the paragraph does not have to be LOOP. It is chosen because it describes the paragraph's function.

The statement PERFORM LOOP 5 TIMES controls the number of times paragraph LOOP is repeated. After PERFORM LOOP 5 TIMES has been executed, control passes to the statement following the PERFORM. In this case, control passes to GO TO NEXT-BIT. If the statement GO TO NEXT-BIT was omitted from the program, then control would pass to LOOP, and LOOP would be executed a sixth time. It is sometimes useful to think of PERFORM as meaning 'go there, do it, then come back'.

An important point about our choice for paragraph names is that no paragraph name should be the same as a COBOL reserved word. From now on we shall include a number with each paragraph name, and place our paragraphs in numerical order. This makes it easy for us to locate a particular paragraph among many paragraphs. Paragraph names in COBOL programs should not contain spaces. Bearing these points in mind, our COBOL algorithm becomes

```
PROCEDURE DIVISION.
010-LOOP-CONTROL.
    MOVE 0 TO W-WEEKLY-TOTAL
    PERFORM 020-LOOP 5 TIMES
    GO TO 030-NEXT-BIT.

020-LOOP.
    DISPLAY "Next daily total"
    ACCEPT W-DAILY-TOTAL
    ADD W-DAILY-TOTAL TO W-WEEKLY-TOTAL.

030-NEXT-BIT.
    DISPLAY "Total for the week is : " W-WEEKLY-TOTAL
    STOP RUN.
```

There are other ways of translating a repeat n times . . . loop into COBOL. We shall stick to this translation because it closely follows the structured English.

Exercise 2.3

1(a)   Complete and test the COBOL program started above, which accumulates the value of goods sold for each day to produce the total for the week. Use whole numbers for pounds instead of decimal numbers for pounds and pence. Test your completed COBOL program with small, simple values.

1(b) Remove the GO TO 030-NEXT-BIT sentence in paragraph 010-LOOP-CONTROL and retest your program. Remember to insert a full stop after PERFORM 020-LOOP 5 TIMES, to mark the end of the paragraph.

2.3.2 WHILE . . . DO . . . ENDWHILE

This algorithm counts the number of names in a list of names. The last item in the list is *** and is not included in the count.

```
        number-of-names ← 0
        read name
        while (name not = ***) do
                add 1 to number-of-names
                read next name
        endwhile
        write number-of-names
        stop
```

In COBOL we might write

```
        PROCEDURE DIVISION.
        010-LOOP-CONTROL.
            MOVE 0 TO W-NUMBER-OF-NAMES
            DISPLAY "Enter a list of names."
            DISPLAY "To end your list enter ***"
            DISPLAY "First name?"
            ACCEPT W-NAME
            PERFORM 020-LOOP UNTIL (W-NAME = "***")
            GO TO 030-NEXT-BIT.

        020-LOOP.
            ADD 1 TO W-NUMBER-OF-NAMES
            DISPLAY "Next name?"
            ACCEPT W-NAME.

        030-NEXT-BIT.
            DISPLAY "The number of names is " W-NUMBER-OF-NAMES
            STOP RUN.
```

The statements to be executed repeatedly are bracketed between do and endwhile; also, they are contained in paragraph 020-LOOP.

The condition for executing the loop is (name not = ***). The condition for not executing i.e. terminating the loop is (name = ***). Therefore, the structured English

```
        while (name not = ***) do {condition for executing the loop}
```

becomes the COBOL

```
        PERFORM ... UNTIL (W-NAME = "***")
        { condition for terminating the loop }
```

In COBOL, the condition for terminating the loop is *only* tested at the *beginning* or the top of the loop. The same is true in structured English. If the condition for terminating the loop becomes met part way through the loop, the remaining statements in the loop are *still executed*.

The following COBOL fragment

```
ACCEPT W-NAME
PERFORM 020-LOOP UNTIL (W-NAME = "***")
statement following the perform comes here
```

means

Get the first name from the program user.
Check the name: as long as the name is NOT equal to ***, repeatedly carry out the statements in 020-LOOP (the last statement in 020-LOOP gets the next name) but before each repetition, check whether the name is still NOT equal to ***.
If the name is equal to ***, then execute the statement following the PERFORM.

Exercise 2.4

1 Complete the COBOL program, started above, which counts the number of names in a list of names. The last item in the list is to be *** and is not to be included in the count.

Note:
(a) Suitable test data might be
      (i) *** { no names — expected result: number of names is 0 }
      (ii) Sue, *** { expected result: number of names is 1 }
      (iii) Sue, Fred, *** { expected result: number of names is 2 }
(b) A data value belonging to W-NAME would contain letters of the alphabet and could contain a hyphen or an apostrophe. If we suppose that 25 character spaces are sufficient for most names, an appropriate declaration in WORKING-STORAGE might be

```
DATA DIVISION.
WORKING-STORAGE SECTION.
01  W-NUMBER-OF-NAMES   PIC 999.
01  W-NAME              PIC X(25).
```

2.4 ARITHMETIC

This algorithm shows how VAT (Value Added Tax) may be calculated on a bill.

```
read bill
calculate vat = 0.15 x bill { 15% = 15/100 = 0.15 }
calculate bill-with-vat = bill + vat
write bill-with-vat
stop
```

We might write this in COBOL as

```
PROCEDURE DIVISION.
010-VAT-CALCULATION.
    DISPLAY "Value of bill?"
    ACCEPT W-BILL
    COMPUTE W-VAT = 0.15 * W-BILL
    COMPUTE W-BILL-WITH-VAT = W-BILL + W-VAT
    DISPLAY "Bill with VAT is : " W-BILL-WITH-VAT
    STOP RUN.
```

COMPUTE means calculate. Notice that there is a space before and after equal signs, and before and after addition and multiplication signs. (* means multiply — unless it appears in column 7, where it signifies a comment line.) In COBOL, the division symbol is /. So, A divided by B would be written A / B. We work our way through some typical calculations.

Suppose W-BILL has the value 100 (pounds).

Then   W-VAT $= 0.15 \times 100$
                                        $= 15$ (pounds)
So   W-BILL-WITH-VAT $= 100 + 15$
                                        $= 115$ (pounds)

Again, suppose W-BILL has the value 16.37 (pounds).

Then   W-VAT $= 0.15 \times 16.37$
                                        $= 2.4555$ (pounds)
So   W-BILL-WITH-VAT $= 16.37 + 2.4555$
                                        $= 18.8255$ (pounds)

We require that the 18.8255 be rounded off to 18.83. So, in COBOL we write

```
COMPUTE W-BILL-WITH-VAT ROUNDED = W-BILL + W-VAT
```

Further, suppose W-BILL has the value 999.99 (pounds).

Then   W-VAT $= 0.15 \times 999.99$
                                        $= 149.9985$ (pounds)
So   W-BILL-WITH-VAT $= 999.99 + 149.9985$
                                        $= 1149.9985$ (pounds)

This last calculation helps us to decide on appropriate sizes for our data items declared in WORKING-STORAGE.

```
DATA DIVISION.
WORKING-STORAGE SECTION.
01   W-BILL                 PIC 999V99.
01   W-VAT                  PIC 999V9999.
01   W-BILL-WITH-VAT        PIC 9999V99.
01   W-BILL-WITH-VAT-OUT    PIC 9999.99.
```

Notice that the variable W-VAT has four digits after the decimal place. (The decimal place is indicated by the V). This is sufficient to maintain accuracy in the intermediate calculation.

We now focus our attention on

```
01   W-BILL-WITH-VAT        PIC 9999V99.
01   W-BILL-WITH-VAT-OUT    PIC 9999.99.
```

01   W-BILL-WITH-VAT   PIC 9999V99. means that the variable can contain a value comprising four digits followed by two further digits. The V stands for virtual decimal point. Its position in a set of 9s in a PICTURE clause indicates the position where a decimal point ought to be. If the statement

```
DISPLAY W-BILL-WITH-VAT
```

is executed, then a decimal point would not appear in the number DISPLAYed.

On the other hand, if a data name contains a decimal point in its definition, as in 01   W-BILL-WITH-VAT-OUT   PIC 9999.99. for example, then this is an actual decimal point. The execution of

```
DISPLAY W-BILL-WITH-VAT-OUT
```

prints the value of the decimal number contained by this variable, with the decimal point actually appearing in the right place.

The statement

```
MOVE W-BILL-WITH-VAT TO W-BILL-WITH-VAT-OUT
```

copies the current value of W-BILL-WITH-VAT into W-BILL-WITH-VAT-OUT, and, in doing so, forces this value into the format specified by W-BILL-WITH-VAT-OUT.

Unfortunately, a variable containing an explicit decimal point in its definition cannot be the subject of an arithmetic process like addition or subtraction, nor can it be the subject of an ACCEPT statement where a decimal value is concerned.

The modified COBOL algorithm is

```
PROCEDURE DIVISION.
010-VAT-CALCULATION.
    DISPLAY "Value of bill?
    ACCEPT W-BILL
    COMPUTE W-VAT = 0.15 * W-BILL
    COMPUTE W-BILL-WITH-VAT ROUNDED = W-BILL + W-VAT
    MOVE W-BILL-WITH-VAT TO W-BILL-WITH-VAT-OUT
    DISPLAY "Bill with VAT is : " W-BILL-WITH-VAT-OUT
    STOP RUN.
```

Exercise 2.5

1(a)   Devise a set of simple values for W-BILL to test the VAT calculator program outlined above. For each of these values, state the result which should be produced. Then, using the test data you have devised, produce a working program.

1(b)   State the conditions under which your program will not produce reasonable results. For example, what happens if the letter I is input instead of the digit 1? What happens if a negative number is input?

2   The following COBOL program prints a fahrenheit–centigrade table.

0	−17.8
20	−6.7
40	4.4
.	.
.	.
300	148.9

For each value of fahrenheit, from 0 to 300 in steps of 20, a value for centigrade is calculated, and the values of fahrenheit and centigrade are printed.

```
* This program prints a fahrenheit-centigrade table
  IDENTIFICATION DIVISION.
  PROGRAM-ID. TM23.

  ENVIRONMENT DIVISION.

  DATA DIVISION.
  WORKING-STORAGE SECTION.
  01   W-BRACKET1   PIC S999.
  01   W-BRACKET2   PIC V9999994.
  01   W-CENT       PIC S999V9.
  01   W-CENT-OUT   PIC ----9.9.
  01   W-FAHR       PIC 999.
  01   W-FAHR-OUT   PIC ZZ9.

  PROCEDURE DIVISION.
  010-LOOP-CONTROL.
       MOVE 0 TO W-FAHR
       PERFORM 020-LOOP UNTIL (W-FAHR > 300)
       STOP RUN.

  020-LOOP.
  *    { The formula is cent = (5.0 / 9.0) * (fahr - 32.0) }
       SUBTRACT 32 FROM W-FAHR GIVING W-BRACKET1
       DIVIDE 5.0 BY 9.0 GIVING W-BRACKET2
       MULTIPLY W-BRACKET1 BY W-BRACKET2 GIVING W-CENT ROUNDED
       MOVE W-CENT TO W-CENT-OUT
       MOVE W-FAHR TO W-FAHR-OUT
       DISPLAY W-FAHR-OUT, "   ", W-CENT-OUT
       ADD 20 TO W-FAHR.
```

Note:
(a) Minus signs are used in place of 9s in

```
  01   W-CENT-OUT   PIC ----9.9.
```

if W-CENT has the value −0034, the effect of

```
  MOVE W-CENT TO W-CENT-OUT
  DISPLAY W-CENT-OUT
```

is to display −3.4. The minus signs replace leading zeroes with spaces, except for the zero immediately before the first significant digit: this zero is replaced with a minus sign.

(b) Zs are used in place of 9s in

```
  01   W-FAHR-OUT   PIC ZZ9.
```

If W-FAHR has the value 005, the effect of

```
  MOVE W-FAHR TO W-FAHR-OUT
  DISPLAY W-FAHR-OUT
```

is to display 5. Z's replace leading zeroes with spaces.

(a) Modify the program so that it prints a heading above each column.
(b) Investigate the effect of changing W-BRACKET2   PIC V9999999. to W-BRACKET   PIC V999. Explain your results.
(c) Write a program to print a centigrade–fahrenheit table for values of centigrade from 0 to 100 in steps of 10.

3

Arrays

3.1 INTRODUCTION

In previous chapters we have referred to various lists e.g. list of names with exam marks. If such a list could be held in a computer's memory, then the computer could do various tasks on the list, such as locate a particular item in the list, or sort the items into alphabetical or numerical order. How can we get a list into a computer's memory?

3.2 THE ARRAY CONCEPT

We start by considering just a list of names.

Green, Smith, Patel, Lyons, Baker

The list-of-names comprises five entries. Each entry is a name. So we have the *data structure*

list-of-names
    name   repeated 5 times

Such a data structure is an example of an *array*.

Translating this data structure into COBOL, and assuming that twenty characters are sufficient for most names, we obtain

```
DATA DIVISION.
WORKING-STORAGE SECTION.
01  W-LIST-OF-NAMES.
    02  W-NAME  PIC X(20)  OCCURS 5 TIMES.
```

The numbers 01 and 02 are called levels. They indicate that W-NAME (level 02) is a part of W-LIST-OF-NAMES (level 01).

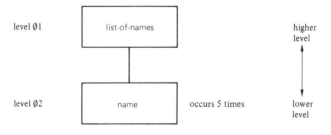

The OCCURS clause cannot be used with a level 01 data name.

The effect of this array declaration is to reserve and label the appropriate space in the computer's memory.

An array has one or more adjacent memory locations or cells. Each cell has an address or number. We can imagine the array as

list-of-names

1	2	3	4	5

name

If the array was filled with names we could visualise

list-of-names

1	2	3	4	5
Green	Smith	Patel	Lyons	Baker

name

How can we examine the contents of a particular memory cell? We could use a variable to locate its position. We shall give this variable the name position. (Some people prefer to use other names, such as subscript, sub, index or pointer.) If position has the value 4, then it refers to the cell whose address is 4,

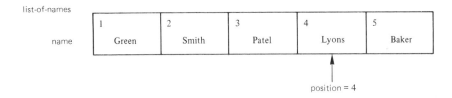

list-of-names

1	2	3	4	5
Green	Smith	Patel	Lyons	Baker

name

position = 4

and name[4] refers to the contents of the memory cell whose address is 4, i.e. to Lyons. So, if position = 2, then name[position] = Smith.

How can we fill the array with names? One way is to assign each name to its position in the array.

    name[1] ← Green
    name[2] ← Smith
    name[3] ← Patel
    name[4] ← Lyons
    name[5] ← Baker

In COBOL we write

```
PROCEDURE DIVISION.
010-FILL-ARRAY.
    MOVE "Green" TO W-NAME (1)
    MOVE "Smith" TO W-NAME (2)
    MOVE "Patel" TO W-NAME (3)
    MOVE "Lyons" TO W-NAME (4)
    MOVE "Baker" TO W-NAME (5).
```

Notice the space between W-NAME and the bracket.

But how can we tell whether the array has been successfully created? We could instruct the computer to display the contents of the array.

```
        position ← 0
        repeat 5 times
                add 1 to position
                write name[position]
        endrepeat
        stop
```

When position has the value 1, name[1] i.e. Green is displayed. When position has the value 2, name[2] i.e. Smith is displayed. When position has the value 3, name[3] . . . etc.

The complete COBOL program, to fill an array with five names and then display them, is

```
        IDENTIFICATION DIVISION.
        PROGRAM-ID. TM31.

        ENVIRONMENT DIVISION.

        DATA DIVISION.
        WORKING-STORAGE SECTION.
        01  W-LIST-OF-NAMES.
                02  W-NAME  PIC X(20)   OCCURS 5 TIMES.
        01  W-POSITION  PIC 9.

        PROCEDURE DIVISION.
        010-FILL-ARRAY.
            MOVE "Green" TO W2-NAME (1)
            MOVE "Smith" TO W2-NAME (2)
            MOVE "Patel" TO W2-NAME (3)
            MOVE "Lyons" TO W2-NAME (4)
            MOVE "Baker" TO W2-NAME (5).

        020-OUTPUT-LOOP-CONTROL.
            DISPLAY "The contents of the array are:"
            MOVE 0 TO W-POSITION
            PERFORM 030-OUTPUT-LOOP 5 TIMES
            GO TO 040-END.

        030-OUTPUT-LOOP.
            ADD 1 TO W-POSITION
            DISPLAY W-NAME (W-POSITION).

        040-END.
            STOP RUN.
```

Exercise 3.1

1 Enter and test program TM31, as shown above.

3.3 GENERALISATIONS

The algorithms to load and output the contents of an array could be made more useful if we allowed the program user to fill the array with names of his or her choice. (A program user is not necessarily a programmer.) The following algorithm achieves this.

```
position ← 0
repeat 5 times
        add 1 to position
        read next-name
        name[position] ← next-name
endrepeat
stop
```

When position has the value 1, a copy of the first name entered is placed in the first position in the array. When position has the value 2, a copy of the next name is placed in the second position in the array. When position has the value 3, a copy of the next name is . . . etc. Translating this algorithm into COBOL we obtain

```
PROCEDURE DIVISION.
010-INPUT-LOOP-CONTROL.
    MOVE 0 TO W-POSITION
    PERFORM 020-INPUT-LOOP 5 TIMES
    GO TO 030-STOP.

020-INPUT-LOOP.
    ADD 1 TO W-POSITION
    DISPLAY "Name?"
    ACCEPT W-NAME (W-POSITION).

030-STOP.
    STOP RUN.
```

The algorithms to load and output the contents of an array could be made even more useful if we refer to LISTSIZE instead of the specific value 5. (In the context of structured English, data names that have a value which remains constant are usually written in upper case. We shall adopt this convention.)

```
load-array
        position ← 0
        repeat LISTSIZE times
                add 1 to position
                read next-name
                name[position] ← next-name
        endrepeat

output-array
        position ← 0
        repeat LISTSIZE times
                add 1 to position
                write name[position]
        endrepeat
```

By referring to LISTSIZE instead of the specific value 5, the algorithm is appropriate for a list of any size — provided that LISTSIZE has a value assigned to it. One way of doing this in COBOL is to write, in the WORKING-STORAGE SECTION, something like

```
DATA DIVISION.
WORKING-STORAGE SECTION.
01  W-LIST-OF-NAMES.
        02  W-NAME    PIC X(20)   OCCURS 5 TIMES.
01  W-LISTSIZE   PIC 9       VALUE 5.
01  W-POSITION   PIC 9
```

Then, if the size of the list was to be changed e.g. from five elements to ten, we need only locate and change three lines: the two lines which refer specifically to a list size of 5, namely

```
        02  W-NAME    PIC X(20)   OCCURS 5 TIMES.
    01  W-LISTSIZE    PIC 9       VALUE 5.
```

and the line specifying the maximum value of W-POSITION, namely

```
    01  W-POSITION  PIC 9.
```

Exercise 3.2

1 Design and write a COBOL program which will
   (a) create and fill an array with five names chosen by the program user
   (b) display the contents of the array.
   Note: 'design and write' means design the data structures and the algorithm in structured English, then translate the data structures and the algorithm into COBOL.

2 Modify the program designed in the previous exercise so that it will
   (a) create and fill an array with 10 names
   (b) display the contents of the array.

3 Design, write and test a COBOL program which will
   (a) create and fill an array with ten names
   (b) ask the user to enter a number corresponding to the position of an entry to be displayed. For example, if the third name was to be displayed, the user would enter 3, and the program would display the third name in the array.

When testing your program, you should ensure that the first and last names in the array can be successfully displayed. What happens if you enter the numbers 0 and 11?

3.4 LINEAR SEARCH

What if we need to know whether a particular name is in the list or not? We could search through the list looking at each name in turn.

Initially, before the search begins, we have not found the name. So we set the variable name-is-found to false.

        name-is-found ← false

If we find the name we are looking for, then we set name-is-found to true.

        if (name[position] = required-name) then
            name-is-found ← true
        endif

If we get to the end of the list, and name-is-found still has the value false, then we can conclude that the required-name is not in the list. These are the essential points of the linear search algorithm.

```
search
    name-is-found ← false
    position ← 1
    read required-name
    while (position ← LISTSIZE) do
        if (name[position] not = required-name) then { no match }
            add 1 to position
        otherwise { match made }
            name-is-found ← true
            position ← LISTSIZE + 1 { forces loop termination }
        endif
    endwhile
result-of-search
    if (name-is-found = true) then
        write required-name is in list
    otherwise { name-is-found = false }
        write required-name is not in list
    endif
    stop
```

Suppose we need to know whether Patel was in the following list.

list-of-names

	1	2	3	4	5
name	Green	Smith	Patel	Lyons	Baker

We record the results of stepping through the linear search algorithm.

Initially, LISTSIZE = 5, name-is-found has the value false, position has the value 1, and the required-name is Patel. The condition (position <= LISTSIZE) is met and we enter the while loop.

The item name[position] (Green) is not equal to the required-name (Patel) so we add 1 to position. position is now 2.

The condition (position <= LISTSIZE) is still met, so we enter the top of the loop again.

The item name[position] (Smith) is not equal to the required-name (Patel) so we add 1 to position. position is now 3.

The condition (position <= LISTSIZE) is still met, so we enter the top of the loop again.

The condition (name[position] not = required-name) is not met, so we do the otherwise part of the if . . . sentence. We set name-is-found to true, and position to LISTSIZE + 1. position is now 6.

The condition (position <= LISTSIZE) is now not met. So we exit from the loop and output the result of the search. name-is-found has the value true, so we output that the required-name (Patel) is in the list.

These results are summarised in the following table.

LISTSIZE	name- is-found	position	required- name	position <= LISTSIZE?	name[position] <> required-name?
5	false	1	Patel	1 <= 5? yes	
		2		2 <= 5? yes	Green<>Patel? yes
		3		3 <= 5? yes	Smith<>Patel? yes
	true	6		6 <= 5? no	Patel<>Patel? no

Note: <> means "is not equal to".

Exercise 3.3

1(a)   Stepping through an algorithm and writing down the results of each step is called a *dry run*. Dry run the linear search algorithm for the following cases.
  (i) the required-name is the first one in the list
  (ii) the required-name is the last one in the list (do not make your list very big)
  (iii) the required-name is not in the list.
1(b)   Translate the linear search algorithm into a COBOL program.
If the condition for executing the loop is (position <= 5), then the condition for terminating the loop is (position > 5). So, the structured English

```
while (position <= 5) do
         .
         .
         .
endwhile
```

translates into the COBOL

```
PERFORM ... UNTIL (W-POSITION > 5)
```

The COBOL means: if the value of W-POSITION is more than 5, do not execute the named paragraph (or paragraphs); if the value of W-POSITION is 5 or less, execute the named paragraph (or paragraphs).

1(c)   Test your program.

2   An array is often called a table. Design, write and test a COBOL program which will set up a table containing month names. A month name should be represented by its first three letters in upper case (i.e. in capital letters). Your program should prompt a user to enter the first three letters, in upper case, of a month name, and then your program should display the corresponding month number. What happens if the user enters lower case instead of upper case for a month name abbreviation?

3.5 TABLELINES

Suppose we are required to set up a table of months and days in each month (thirty days hath September, April, June and . . . Assume 28 days in February). A suitable data structure for the table might be

> calendar-table
> > tableline repeated 12 times
> > > month
> > > days-in-month

i.e.

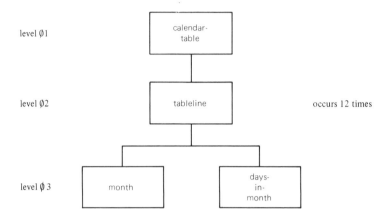

Each line in the table comprises a month and the number of days in that month. There are twelve lines. We represent this in COBOL.

```
WORKING-STORAGE SECTION.
01   W-CALENDAR-TABLE.
       02   W-TABLELINE              OCCURS 12 TIMES.
              03   W-MONTH           PIC X(3).
              03   W-DAYS-IN-MONTH   PIC 99.
```

Now, how can we fill the array with data? One way is to assign the data values directly to the array with MOVE statements. For example:

```
MOVE "JAN" TO W-MONTH (1)
MOVE 31 TO W-DAYS-IN-MONTH (1)
MOVE "FEB" TO W-MONTH (2)
MOVE 28 TO W-DAYS-IN-MONTH (2)
MOVE "MAR" TO W-MONTH (3)
etc.
```

This table would be useful for the following situation:

A program is required which will convert a date in the form day-in-month number, month name to the day-in-year number. For example, if the date input is 3 MAR then the day day-in-year number is 62 (31 for Jan plus 28 for Feb plus 3 for Mar).

The essential idea is much the same as for the linear search. We use a variable line-number to refer to each line of the table in turn. The value of line-number is initially one. Initially, we refer to the first line of the table, namely JAN31. If the month input (month-in) is not the same as the month in the table referenced by line-number (month[line-number]), then add the corresponding days-in-month (days-in-month[line-number]) to the count of days (day-count). Otherwise, if month-in is the same as month[linenumber], then add the day input (day-in) to day-count and terminate the loop. Finally, output the value of day-count i.e. the day number in the year.

```
find-day-in-year
    input day-in, month-in
    day-count ← 0
    line-number ← 1
    while (line-number <= 12) do
        if (month-in not = month[line-number]) then
            add day[line-number] to day-count
            add 1 to line-number
        otherwise
            add day-in to day-count
            line-number ← 13 { forces loop termination }
        endif
    endwhile
    output day-count
    stop
```

Exercise 3.4

1(a) What is the day-in-year number in a non leap year corresponding to the following dates?
  (i) 1 JAN { first day in the year }
  (ii) 31 DEC { last day in the year }
  (iii) 15 JUN { middle of the year — approximately }

1(b) Dry run the find-day-in-year algorithm using the dates given in **1(a),** above. Implement the find-day-in-year algorithm in COBOL. Assume that only reasonable values for the day and month name are input, and that there are 28 days in February.

2 A year is a leap year if it can be divided by four without remainder, unless the year is also exactly divisible by 100 but not by 400. For example,

1984 is a leap year   { divisible by 4 without remainder }
1900 is not a leap year   { divisible by 100 without remainder }
2000 is a leap year   { divisible by 400 without remainder }

Design and write a program which will accept four digits and then display whether or not it is a leap year.

3 Now modify the program you wrote for Exercise 3.4, number 1, so that it will input a date in the form day-number, month-name, year-number and output the day number in the year. If the year is a leap year, then February has 29 days — use a separate array, called leap-calendar-table, say, which contains the first three letters of each month name together with the days in each month in a leap year.

4 Design, write and completely test a COBOL program which will
  (a) create and load a table with month names and the number of days in each month (assume that February has 28 days)
  (b) input a date in the form day-number, month-name
  (c) test the day-number input: if the day-number input is less than one or more than the number of days in month-name, then output the message "day is not valid"; otherwise output "day is ok"
  (d) test the month-name input: if the month-name input is not in the table of month names, then output the message "month is not valid"; otherwise output "month is ok".

4
Testing

4.1 INTRODUCTION

If we dry run an algorithm with data deliberately designed to show that it works as intended, we can say that our algorithm is *probably* correct: we can say no more than this. Choosing data values to test an algorithm is an important part of the program design process. In this chapter, we look at strategies for choosing test data.

4.2 CHOOSING TEST DATA

Strategies for choosing test data are suggested by programming experience. We focus our attention on situations where errors are likely to occur.

The following is a simple algorithm to process an exam mark.

```
read exam-mark
if (exam-mark < 40) then
    write "fail"
otherwise
    write "pass"
endif
```

Appropriate data values for testing this algorithm are 39, 40 and 41 because they are close to the critical value, 40. Forty is the critical value because an exam mark just less than forty would result in fail being displayed, and an exam mark of exactly forty, or just more than forty, would result in pass being displayed. We can represent this on a number line.

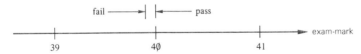

In this example, forty represents a boundary value: it represents the boundary between pass and fail. We consider choosing as test data values which fall just either side of a boundary, and exactly on the boundary. Boundaries represent situations where program design errors are most likely to occur. Boundaries can be found in loops, arithmetical formulae and in lists.

With a loop, we choose data values which would cause the loop to be executed (a) not at all and (b) at least once.

We choose both very large and very small values, zero and negative values for variables when a formula is involved. For example, a formula for calculating the average of a number of exam marks is

$$average \leftarrow \frac{total\text{-}exam\text{-}mark}{number\text{-}of\text{-}exam\text{-}marks}$$

In choosing test data for this formula, we would consider various combinations of

(a)	very large value for total-exam-mark
(b)	very large value for number-of-exam-marks
(c)	very small value for total-exam-marks
(d)	very small value for number-of-exam-marks
(e)	total-exam-mark = 0
(f)	number-of-exam-marks = 0
(g)	total-exam-mark = -1
(h)	number-of-exam-marks = -1

When processing a list of items, we pay special attention to the very first and the very last item in the list. We also consider the possibility that the list has no items whatsoever.

The following examples help illustrate how we might go about choosing test data.

4.2.1 ARRAYS AS ACCUMULATORS

Suppose we have a large list of exam candidates and their marks (the marks are between 0 and 100 inclusive) and we want to know how many candidates obtained 100 marks, how many candidates obtained 99 marks, how many obtained 98 marks, how many obtained 97 marks, and so on for each possible mark down to 0. An outline of what we need to do is

```
for each candidate
        read the mark
        add 1 to the appropriate mark-counter
endfor
for each mark-counter
        output its value
endfor
```

How could we add one to the appropriate mark-counter? We could write something like

```
if (mark = 0) then
        add 1 to 0-mark-counter
endif
if (mark = 1) then
        add 1 to 1-mark-counter
endif
if (mark = 2) then
        add 1 to 2-mark-counter
endif
if (mark = 3) then
        add 1 to 3-mark-counter

        .
        .
and so on.
```

But this is very tedious and inefficient.

A better method would be to use an array in which each element corresponds to a mark-counter. We investigate this idea by first limiting our range of marks, just to make the problem manageable.

Suppose that the only possible marks are 1, 2, 3, 4 and 5. We want to know how many students scored 1 mark, how many scored 2 marks, how many scored 3, etc.

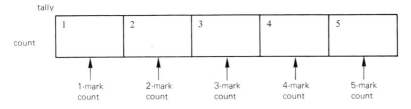

Suppose the list of marks for ten students is

2, 5, 2, 1, 5, 3, 4, 2, 2, 1

and that our outline algorithm is

        for each student
            read mark
            count[mark] ← count[mark] + 1

Initially, all the counters have value **0**.

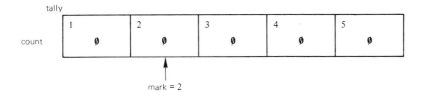

We read the first mark. It is 2. If we use mark to refer to a position in the array we obtain

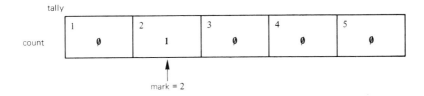

The next statement, count[mark] ← count[mark] + 1 becomes

        count[2] ← count[2] + 1

This adds 1 to the contents of count[2].

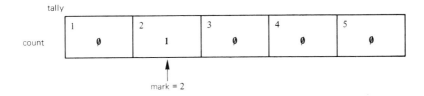

We read the next mark. It is 5. We add 1 to count[5].

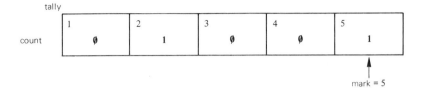

We read the next mark. It is 2. We add 1 to count[2].

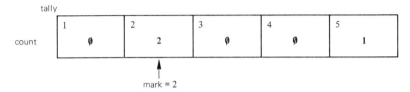

And so on until all the marks have been read and the appropriate counters updated. The final tally looks like:

tally

1	2	3	4	5
count 2	4	1	1	2

To find, for example, how many students scored two marks, we need only execute

```
mark ← 2
write count[mark]
```

to obtain the answer, four.

The following algorithm initialises the count array, keeps a tally of the marks which are input and then outputs the tally.

```
tally
    mark ← 1                        { initialises count array }
    while (mark <= MAXMARK) do { MAXMARK = 5 in our example }
        count[mark] ← 0
        mark ← mark + 1
    endwhile

    input mark                      { fills count array }
    while (mark not = -1) do        { -1 terminates input }
        count[mark] ← count[mark] + 1
        input mark
    endwhile

    mark ← 1                        { outputs contents of count array }
    while (mark <= MAXMARK) do
        output count[mark]
        mark ← mark + 1
    endwhile
```

Now what about the test data? The first loop, which initialises the count array, does not generate any test data. We merely have to satisfy ourselves that the first five elements are each assigned the value zero. This we can do with a dry run.

What marks should we use to test the input loop? We want to execute the loop (a) not at all and (b) at least once. Therefore we choose (a) -1 and (b) 1, -1. These two sets of marks constitute two test cases. We can summarise our choice in a table.

Test case	Test data	Effect
1	-1	input loop not executed
2	1, -1	input loop executed at least once

The second test case also adds one to the value of count[1] — the first element in the count array. The last element in the count array can be incremented if we choose five as test value. We need modify only test case two to include it.

Test case	Test data	Effect
1	-1	input loop not executed
2	1,5,-1	execute input loop at least once increment first and last count

An important part of choosing test data is predicting the outcome of our choice. These predictions can then be compared with the results actually obtained when the algorithm is executed. Only then can we decide whether our algorithm is probably correct. Test data and predictions together form a test plan.

Test Plan

Test case	Test data	Reason	Expected result
1	-1	input loop not executed	number of 1s: 0 number of 2s: 0 number of 3s: 0 number of 4s: 0 number of 5s: 0
2	1,5,-1	execute input loop increment first and last	number of 1s: 1 number of 2s: 0 number of 3s: 0 number of 4s: 0 number of 5s: 1

Data values of one and five represent the smallest and largest mark that the algorithm can process i.e. boundaries. What about marks of zero and six? Either we modify the algorithm so that it deals sensibly with any data input for a mark, no matter how unreasonable that data might be. (For example the letters I or O might count as unreasonable data.) Or we state that our algorithm cannot process such data — and leave it at that.

A statement of the limitations of a program is an important piece of documentation. It could be included in a Program Documentation Page. Such a page could comprise

> program name — the PROGRAM-IDentity entry
> usage – the program name held by the disk directory
> function – a statement of what the program does
> example – of one program run
> limitations – what the program cannot process i.e. instances when
> the program will fail

The document page should be typed (by using a word processor for example).

Exercise 4.1

1   Design, write, test and document a program which will count and output the number of students that obtained each possible mark from a large list of students' exam marks in the range 0 to 10 inclusive.
Note:
(a)   In COBOL, an array cannot have an element whose address is 0. Therefore, you will need to treat a mark of 0 as a special case.
(b)   Your documentation should include
> algorithm in structured English
> test plan
> program documentation page
> program listing — as output from the compiler
> program runs — with the data specified in the test plan.

Your algorithm, test plan and program documentation page should be typed.

4.2.2 BINARY CHOP OR LOGARITHMIC SEARCH

Searching through a list, one item at a time, can be very time consuming, especially if the list is large. A linear search is not an efficient method of locating an item in a list. A more efficient method might be to chop the list in half repeatedly until the required item is found. With this method, the items must be held in the list in alphabetical or numerical order, and there must be no repetitions (i.e. no two items can have the same value).

Suppose we want to locate the number **41** in the following list of numbers.

	1	2	3	4	5	6	7	8	9
list	22	24	27	33	36	39	41	44	47

We use three variables to refer to, or address, elements of the array. These are first, last and middle.

Initially, first has the value one, last the value nine, and middle the value five. middle divides the list into two halves — the left half and the right half.

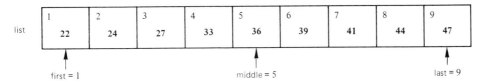

There are three possibilities. Either the number-sought is equal to the value of list[middle], or it is less than list[middle], or it is greater than list[middle].

The number-sought (**44**) is not equal to the value of list[middle] (**36**), nor is it less than list[middle]. But number-sought is greater than list[middle], so we discard the left half of the list, including the middle.

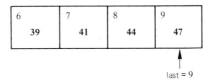

and we adjust the values of first and middle.

    first ← middle + 1
    middle ← (first +last)/2 { rounded down }

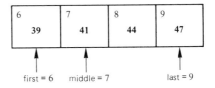

The number-sought (**41**) is equal to list[middle] (**41**), so we terminate the search. Here is the logarithmic search, binary chop or binary search algorithm.

```
binary-search
    input number-sought
    item-is-found ← false
    first ← 1
    last ← LISTSIZE { in our example, LISTSIZE = 9 }
    middle ← (first + last)/2 { rounded down if necessary }

    while (first < = last) do
        if (number-sought = list[middle]) then
            item-is-found←true
            first ← LIST SIZE + 1
        else if (number-sought < list[middle]) then
            { discard right half }
            last ← middle - 1
            middle ← (first + last)/2 { rounded down }
        else if (number-sought > list[middle]) then
            { discard left half }
            first ← middle + 1
            middle ← (first + last)/2 {rounded down}
        endif
    endwhile
```

Notice the if . . . else if . . . else if . . . construction. The American word 'else' is used instead of the English word 'otherwise' (both mean the same thing) and the elses are aligned one under the other. Suppose, for example, number-sought = 27 and list[middle] = 36. The first condition (number-sought = list[middle]) is tested; it is not met. The second condition (number-sought < list[middle]) is tested; it is met. So the corresponding statement block

```
last ← middle − 1
middle ← (first + last)/2
```

is executed and control is passed directly to endif. The third condition (number-sought > list[middle]) is bypassed; it is not tested.

In general, when a chain of else ifs is executed, each condition is tested in turn until one is met; then the corresponding statement block is executed, the remaining conditions bypassed and control passed to the end of the construction. At most, only one block of statements, corresponding to the first condition that is met, is executed.

All that remains now is to output the results of the search.

```
result-of-search
      if (item-is-found = true) then
            output number-sought is in list
      else (if item-is-found = false) then
            output number-sought is not in list
      endif
```

We consider the following points when drawing up the test plan (p. 37)

We choose to locate the first and last items in the list — the boundary items. Also, we choose a data value just less than the first, and just greater than the last item in the list.

We are repeatedly dividing the list in half. Therefore we choose lists with (a) an odd number of elements and (b) an even number of elements.

We want to execute the search loop (a) not at all and (b) once.

The binary search algorithm has two important limitations: the elements must be in alphabetical or numerical order, and no two elements can be the same.

Exercise 4.2

1 Test and document a COBOL program which will efficiently search through an ordered list of unique four-figure account numbers.

4.2.3 SORTING USING ARRAYS (BUBBLE SORT)

Suppose we wish to sort the following list of names into alphabetical order.

	1	2	3	4	5
name	TOM	DICK	HARRY	VICKY	MAY

Basically, we compare adjacent elements; if they are not in alphabetical order, we swap the positions of the data items. We repeat this until all the data items are in order.

Test Plan

Test case	Test data	Reason	Expected result
1.	list comprises 9 items 22,24,27,33,36,39,41,44,47	odd number of items	
	number-sought		
(a)	21	boundaries of list	item not found
(b)	22		item found
(c)	47		item found
(d)	48		item not found
2.	list comprises 8 items 22,24,27,33,36,39,41,44	even number of items	
	number-sought		
(a)	21	boundaries of list	item not found
(b)	22		item found
(c)	44		item found
(d)	45		item not found
3.	list comprises 0 items	search loop not executed	
	number-sought		
(a)	20		item not found
4.	list comprises 1 item, 20	search loop executed once	
	number-sought		
(a)	20		item found
(b)	21		item not found

We use the variables current and next to refer to, or address elements of the array, and the variable is-sorted to indicate when sorting is complete.

Initially current has the value one, next has the value two, and is-sorted the value true. We assume that all is in order, unless we find a pair of items that are not.

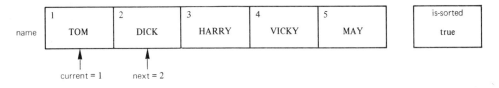

We compare name[current] with name[next]. They are not in order, so we swap their positions, set is-sorted to false, and add one to both current and next.

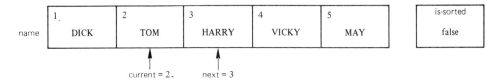

We compare name[current] with name[next]. They are not in order, so we swap their positions and add one to both current and next. is-sorted remains false.

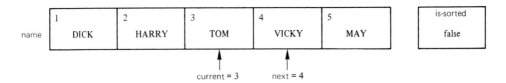

We compare name[current] with name[next]. They are both in alphabetical order. So we move on to the next pair by incrementing both current and next by one.

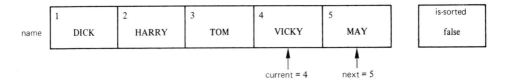

We compare name[current] with name[next]. They are not in order, So we swap their positions and add one to both current and next. is-sorted remains false.

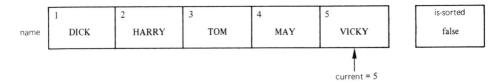

We have now passed once through the list from beginning to end and, in doing so, increased the amount of order in the list i.e. from two adjacent pairs originally (DICK and HARRY, HARRY and VICKY) to three adjacent pairs now (DICK and HARRY, HARRY and TOM, MAY and VICKY). This process is repeated until the list is completely sorted. Proceeding from the beginning to the end of a list is called a *pass*.

At the beginning of each pass, is-sorted is set to true. If it remains true at the end of a pass (because no swaps have been made) then we can conclude that the items in the list are all in alphabetical order.

Interchanging the positions of two data items in an array is easy. We use a variable called store to hold a copy of the next element. Then we copy the current element into the next position. Finally, we copy the item held in store into the current position. Thus:

		name [current]	name- [next]	store
initially		TOM	DICK	
step 1	store ← name[next]			DICK
step 2	name[next] ← name[current]		TOM	
step 3	name[current] ← store	DICK		

The algorithm for a single pass is shown next.

```
pass
    current ← 1
    next ← current + 1
    is-sorted ← true
    while (current < LISTSIZE) do
        if (name[current] > name[next]) then { not in order }
            is-sorted ← false
            store ← name[next]              { swop positions }
            name[next] ← name[current]
            name[curent] ← store
        endif
        current ← current + 1
        next ← next + 1
    endwhile
```

Passes are repeated while the list remains unsorted.

```
    while (is-sorted = false) do
            pass
    endwhile
```

The complete algorithm is

```
sort
    is-sorted ← false
    while (is-sorted = false) do
            current ← 1                                  { pass through the list }
            next ← current + 1
            is-sorted ← true
            while (current < LISTSIZE) do               { check each pair }
                if (name[current] < name[next]) then        { not in order }
                    is-sorted ← false
                    store ← name[next]                  { swop positions }
                    name[next] ← name[current]
                    name[current] ← store
                endif
                current ← current + 1
                next ← next + 1
            endwhile
    endwhile
```

Now what about the test data? Since the algorithm is supposed to sort a list of names into alphabetical order, it should be able to process

(a) a list in which no names are in order. for example, E,D,C,B,A
and (b) a list in which all names are in order. for example, A,B,C,D,E.

It also should be able to sort a list in which all names are identical, (e.g. A,A,A,A,A) a list which contains one name (LISTSIZE = 1) and a list which contains no names whatsoever (LISTSIZE = 0).

```
030-SORT-CONTROL.
    MOVE "FALSE" TO W-IS-SORTED
    PERFORM 040-SORT-LOOP UNTIL (W-IS-SORTED = "TRUE")
    GO TO 060-NEXT-BIT.

040-SORT-LOOP.
    MOVE 1 TO W-CURRENT
    ADD 1 W-CURRENT GIVING W-NEXT
    MOVE "TRUE" TO W-IS-SORTED
    PERFORM 050-PASS UNTIL (W-CURRENT = W-LISTSIZE).

050-PASS.
    IF (W-NAME (W-CURRENT) > W-NAME (W-NEXT))
        MOVE "FALSE" TO W-IS-SORTED
        MOVE W-NAME (W-NEXT) TO W-STORE
        MOVE W-NAME (W-CURRENT) TO W-NAME (W-NEXT)
        MOVE W-STORE TO W-NAME (W-CURRENT).
    ADD 1 TO W-CURRENT
    ADD 1 TO W-NEXT.

060-NEXT-BIT.
```

Exercise 4.3

1(a)   Dry run the sort algorithm with a list of names of your choice.

1(b)   Draw up a test plan for the sort algorithm given above. Take care when predicting the results for LISTSIZE = 0 and 1.

1(c)   Produce a documented COBOL program which sorts names held in an array into alphabetical order.
Note:
(a) One way of coding the loop within a loop is

Compare this algorithm with the structured English version.
(b) Sorting items into alphabetic order is possible because letters are automatically converted into a numeric code. A code in common use is the American Standard Code for Information Interchange (ASCII). In ASCII, A = 65, B = 66, C = 67, etc. The letter A comes before B because 65 comes before 66.

4.3 STRUCTURAL AND FUNCTIONAL TEST DATA

Test data derived from the algorithm structure is called structural test data. The purpose of structural test data is to execute each statement in an algorithm at least once. A limitation of this strategy for obtaining test data is that it depends on the programmer designing the algorithm correctly in the first place.

Test data derived from the job specification i.e. the job the algorithm was intended to do, is called functional test data. A limitation with this strategy is that the specification may be deficient in some important respects.

In practice, a combination of methods is used to obtain test data. But no matter how carefully we choose test data and test our programs, we can never be certain that our programs are free from all errors. All we can say is that we have not found any errors — so far. Program testing shows the presence of errors, never their absence.

Testing with structural test data is known as glass–box or white–box testing. Testing with functional test data is known as black–box testing.

5
Serial files

5.1 INTRODUCTION

A computer's memory is usually volatile in the sense that if the computer is switched off, then the contents of that memory are destroyed. Arrays, whose structure and contents are held in memory, are not much use for keeping large amounts of data from day to day. To keep a large amount of data always accessible, data is stored in files on external media such as a disk.

5.2 FILES, RECORDS AND FIELDS

Supose the Society for the Protection of Small Mammals holds the following information on each of its subscribing members

> name
> address
> class of membership {this might be 'student' or 'full'}

The information could be held in a book. Part of a page in the book could look something like

NAME	ADDRESS	CLASS
.	.	.
Green, P	99 Burleys Way Ltown	full
Patel, A	39 Coventry Rd Stown	student
Jones, J	2 Leicester Rd Ptown	student
.	.	.
.	.	.

How could the information be put onto a computer file? There are two components to the answer: data structures and algorithms. We look first at the data structure.

The data occurs in a repeating pattern. The pattern comprises

> name, address, class-of-membership

Such a pattern describes a *record*. An example of a record with this pattern is

Patel, A   39 Coventry Rd Stown   student

One or more records constitute a *file*.

name, address and class-of-membership are examples of *fields*. A record comprises one or more fields.

So, we have the data structure

```
members-file
        members-record {repeated one or more times}
                name-field
                address-field
                class-of-membership-field
```

Notice the use of indentation. It shows that the members' file comprises one or more member records. Each record comprises the fields name, address and class-of-membership.

Another way to show this hierarchical structure is by a diagram.

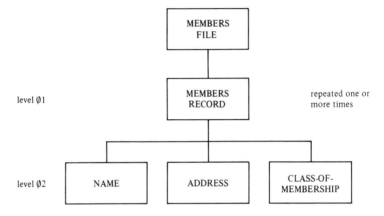

Declaring this file structure in COBOL, and allowing an appropriate number of characters for each field we obtain

```
DATA DIVISION.
FILE SECTION.
FD  MEMBERS-FILE
        LABEL RECORDS ARE STANDARD
        VALUE OF FILE-ID IS "A:MEMBFILE.DAT".
01  SUBSCRIBERS-RECORD.
        02  NAME                    PIC X(25).
        02  ADDRESS                 PIC X(50).
        02  CLASS-OF-MEMBERSHIP  PIC X.
```

If we code "F" for full and "S" for student, then a single character (PIC X) for CLASS-OF-MEMBERSHIP is sufficient.

Files are declared in the FILE SECTION of the DATA DIVISION. FD stands for file definition. LABEL RECORDS ARE STANDARD ensures that the beginning and end of the file on the disk are marked in a way which is recognized by the computer's operating system.

A:MEMBFILE.DAT is the name by which the file is known within the operating system. When the operating system is in control (you see a prompt, something like A>) and you enter a command like dir, this is the name which appears in the disk directory. The A: specifies disk drive A. If your file was to be held on the disk in drive B, then you would write B: before the file name. There should be no spaces between the disk drive name and the file name.

MEMBERS-FILE is the name by which the file is known within the program. The FD entry connects together the external file name, A:MEMBFILE.DAT, with the internal file name, MEMBERS-FILE.

The level numbers 01 and 02 declare that the MEMBERS-RECORD (level 01) comprises the fields (level 02) NAME, ADDRESS AND CLASS-OF-MEMBERSHIP. Incidentally, instead of using level number 02, you could use any number between 02 and 49 inclusive.

The following entries in the ENVIRONMENT DIVISION assign the MEMBERS-FILE to the disk drive (rather than to another device such as a printer or a tape drive).

```
ENVIRONMENT DIVISION.
INPUT-OUTPUT SECTION.
FILE-CONTROL.
      SELECT SUBSCRIBERS-FILE
          ASSIGN TO DISK.
```

5.3 FILE CREATION

The essential idea for file creation is

```
read the data in e.g. from the keyboard
write the record out to the file
```

Here is the algorithm in more detail.

```
members-file-creation
        open members-file for writing out
        get members-name from keyboard
        while (members-name not terminator) do
               get rest of record from keyboard
               write out record to members-file
               get next members-name from keyboard
        endwhile
        close members-file
```

terminator is a special 'name' to indicate that there is no more input.

The following COBOL program achieves the file creation. Notice that we include F1 (for file number one) in the file and associated record and field names. This ensures that no file, record or field name can be identical to a COBOL reserved word. And if we had more than one file, with a different number associated with each file, then no two records or fields from different files can have the same name.

```
*   This program creates a file of subscribers to the
*   Society for the Protection of Small Mammals.

    IDENTIFICATION DIVISION.
    PROGRAM-ID. TM51.
    ENVIRONMENT DIVISION.
    INPUT-OUTPUT SECTION.
    FILE-CONTROL.
        SELECT F1-MEMBERS-FILE
             ASSIGN TO DISK.

    DATA DIVISION.
    FILE SECTION.
    FD F1-MEMBERS-FILE
        LABEL RECORDS ARE STANDARD
        VALUE OF FILE-ID IS "A:MEMBFILE.DAT".
    01  F1-MEMBERS-RECORD.
        05  F1-NAME                  PIC X(20).
        05  F1-ADDRESS               PIC X(50).
        05  F1-CLASS-OF-MEMBERSHIP   PIC X.

    WORKING-STORAGE SECTION.

    PROCEDURE DIVISION.
    010-CONTROL.
        OPEN OUTPUT F1-MEMBERS-FILE
        DISPLAY "Membership file creation."
        DISPLAY "(To end the file creation enter *** for name)"
        DISPLAY "Name?"
        ACCEPT F1-NAME
        PERFORM 020-LOOP UNTIL F1-NAME = "***"
        GO TO 030-CLOSE.

    020-LOOP.
        DISPLAY "Address?"
        ACCEPT F1-ADDRESS
        DISPLAY "Class of membership?"
        ACCEPT F1-CLASS-OF-MEMBERSHIP
        WRITE F1-MEMBERS-RECORD

        DISPLAY "Name?"
        ACCEPT F1-NAME.

    030-CLOSE.
        CLOSE F1-MEMBERS-FILE
        DISPLAY "End of Membership file creation."
        STOP RUN.
```

How can you tell whether the file was successfully created? You could interrogate the disk file directory (e.g. by entering a command like dir when the operating system is in control) and look for the file name entry. But finding the file name in the directory tells you nothing about the contents of the file. One way of determining whether all the data was written to the file is to execute a program to display the contents of that file. Such a program is very similar to the file creation program. The essential difference is that instead of writing records to a file, records are retrieved from the file.

5.4 RECORD RETRIEVAL

The declared file structure in the record retrieval program must, of course, be the same as the declared file structure in the file creation program. The essentials of the record retrieval algorithm are

```
members–record–retrieval
        open members–file for reading in
        retrieve first record
        while (not end-of-file) do
                display record on screen
                retrieve next record
        endwhile
        close members-file
```

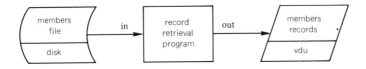

And now turn to the next page for the COBOL program.

```
*   This program displays the contents of the file of
*   subscribers to the Society for the Protection of
*   Small Mammals.

    IDENTIFICATION DIVISION.
    PROGRAM-ID. TM52.
    ENVIRONMENT DIVISION.
    INPUT-OUTPUT SECTION.
    FILE-CONTROL.
        SELECT F1-MEMBERS-FILE
            ASSIGN TO DISK.

    DATA DIVISION.
    FILE SECTION.
    FD F1-MEMBERS-FILE
        LABEL RECORDS ARE STANDARD
        VALUE OF FILE-ID IS "A:MEMBFILE.DAT".
    01  F1-MEMBERS-RECORD.
        02  F1-NAME                   PIC X(20).
        02  F1-ADDRESS                PIC X(50).
        02  F1-CLASS-OF-MEMBERSHIP    PIC X.

    WORKING-STORAGE SECTION.
    01  W-END-OF-FILE                 PIC X(5).

    PROCEDURE DIVISION. ·
    010-CONTROL.
        DISPLAY "Members file."
        OPEN INPUT F1-MEMBERS-FILE
        MOVE "FALSE" TO W-END-OF-FILE
        READ F1-MEMBERS-FILE
            AT END MOVE "TRUE" TO W-END-OF-FILE.
        PERFORM 020-LOOP UNTIL (W-END-OF-FILE = "TRUE")
        GO TO 030-CLOSE.

    020-LOOP.
        DISPLAY F1-MEMBERS-RECORD
        READ F1-MEMBERS-FILE
            AT END MOVE "TRUE" TO W-END-OF-FILE.

    030-CLOSE.
        CLOSE F1-MEMBERS-FILE
        DISPLAY "End of Members File."
        STOP RUN.
```

The file is opened and W-END-OF-FILE is set to FALSE. The READ statement is executed for the first time. Suppose that the file contains one record. Then the end of the file has not been reached and this record is retrieved, i.e. a copy of the record is placed in memory. Then the condition (W-END-OF-FILE = "TRUE") is tested. The condition is not met (because W-END-OF-FILE still has the value FALSE), and so 020-LOOP is entered, the record in memory is displayed, and the file is READ again. Now, the end of the file has been reached, so W-END-OF-FILE is set to TRUE. Control returns to

```
PERFORM 020-LOOP UNTIL (W-END-OF-FILE = "TRUE")
```

The condition (W-END-OF-FILE = "TRUE") is tested. The condition is now met so 020-LOOP is not executed again; instead, the statement

```
GO TO 030-CLOSE
```

is carried out.

The effect of the READ statement is either to detect the end of the file, or, if not at the end of the file, to retrieve the next record and place a copy of it into the computer's memory. If the end of the file has been reached, then the statements between AT END and the next full stop are executed. In this case, there is only one statement: MOVE "TRUE" TO W-END-OF-FILE.

Displaying the contents of a file on the screen is an example of dumping. Files are often dumped to the printer, and this is the subject of the next chapter. Whenever a file is created or its contents changed, a file dump should be carried out to show that the creation or update was successful.

Exercise 5.1

1(a)   Design and write a program which will create a file of owners of bicycles. The file should contain the owner's name and address, and the bicycle frame number.

1(b)   Design and write a program which will display the contents of the owners-of-bicycles file on the screen.

Remember to test and document your programs.

2(a)   Create a mark-file of names and exam marks.

2(b)   Design and write a program which uses this file as its input, and creates a results-file of names and grades. The grades should be obtained from the marks as follows.

mark	0 to 30	31 to 39	40 to 57	58 to 74	75 to 100
grade	fail	refer	pass	credit	distinction

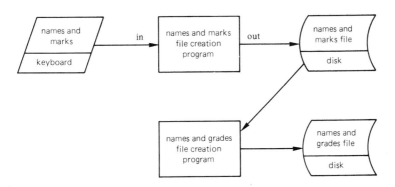

2(c)   Design and write a program which will produce a pass-file and a fail-file from the results-file of candidates and their examination grades. Grades qualifying for the pass-file are pass, credit and distinction. Grades qualifying for the fail-file are fail and refer.

Remember to check the contents of each file.

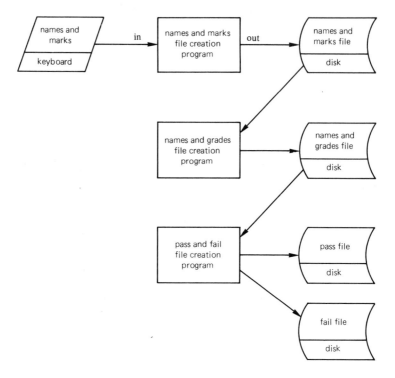

6
Printer Formatting

6.1 INTRODUCTION

In the previous chapter we described how the contents of files could be displayed on the screen. In many cases, e.g. with large records and large files, and where a permanent written copy is required, dumping a file to the screen is inappropriate. A more suitable output device would be a printer. In this chapter we see how to design a print layout and implement it in COBOL.

6.2 PRINTLINE FORMATS

Suppose a table of numbers from one to ten, together with their squares and cubes are to be printed on standard listing paper (eleven inches by eight and a half inches — approximately A4 size).

number	square	cube
1	1	1
2	4	8
3	9	27
4	16	64
5	25	125
6	36	216
7	49	343
8	64	512
9	81	729
10	100	1000

How can we control where each item of output on a line of print appears?

Suppose eighty characters can fit on one line. A printer format sheet or a display chart or graph paper could be used to help determine what is to appear on each line — look at Figure 6.1. Two types of line are involved: a line which contains column headings, and lines which contain numbers. We shall choose the name report-line for a line which contains variables whose values are to be printed.

The line column-headings comprises 29 spaces, followed by "NUMBER", followed by 2 spaces, followed by "SQUARE", followed by 3 spaces, followed by "CUBE", followed by 30 spaces, i.e.

column-headings
    spaces:29, "NUMBER", spaces:2, "SQUARE", spaces:3, "CUBE", spaces:30

The report-line comprises 31 spaces, followed by 2 spaces for the variable number, followed by 5 spaces, followed by 3 spaces for the variable square, followed by 5

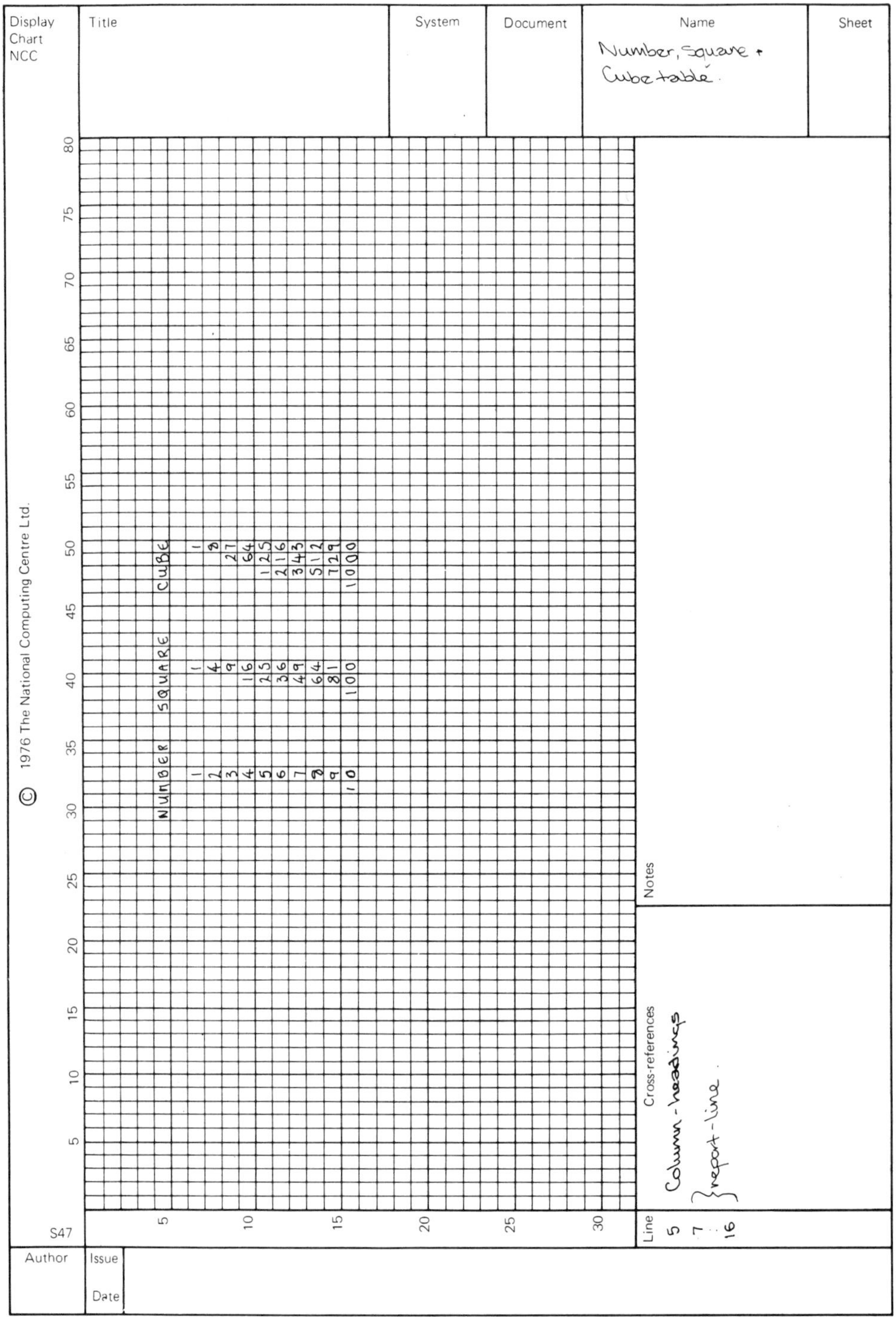

Figure 6.1   Printer format for table of numbers, their squares and cubes

spaces, followed by 4 spaces for the variable cube, followed by 30 spaces. We can express this by writing

report-line
      spaces:31, number:2, spaces:5, square:3, spaces:5, cube:4, spaces:30

The completed display chart is an invaluable aid to designing and defining the printline formats. A printline format describes the composition of a line that is to be output to a printer.

In COBOL, printline formats are defined in the WORKING-STORAGE SECTION of the DATA DIVISION.

```
WORKING-STORAGE SECTION.
01   COLUMN-HEADINGS.
       05   FILLER   PIC X(29)   VALUE SPACES.
       05   FILLER   PIC X(6)    VALUE "NUMBER".
       05   FILLER   PIC XX      VALUE SPACES.
       05   FILLER   PIC X(6)    VALUE "SQUARE".
       05   FILLER   PIC XXX     VALUE SPACES.
       05   FILLER   PIC X(4)    VALUE "CUBE".
       05   FILLER   PIC X(30)   VALUE SPACES.

01   REPORT-LINE.
       05   FILLER     PIC X(31)   VALUE SPACES.
       05   W-NUMBER   PIC Z9.
       05   FILLER     PIC X(5)    VALUE SPACES.
       05   W-SQUARE   PIC ZZ9.
       05   FILLER     PIC X(5)    VALUE SPACES.
       05   W-CUBE     PIC ZZZ9.
       05   FILLER     PIC X(30)   VALUE SPACES.
```

FILLER is the universal data name which we use if we do not need to refer to a data name specifically.

Suppose W-NUMBER was assigned the value 3. If W-NUMBER was defined as PIC 99, then DISPLAY W-NUMBER would result in 03 being printed. If W-NUMBER was defined as PIC Z9, then DISPLAY W-NUMBER would result in 3 being displayed. Where Zs are written in place of leading 9s in a PICTURE statement, leading zeros, if any, are not printed.

W-NUMBER PIC Z9 is an example of an edited field, and Z is an example of an editing character. Editing characters are used to format output. Another example of an editing character is the full stop; this is used to indicate explicitly a decimal point in a number to be printed.

Unfortunately, arithmetic cannot be performed with fields containing editing characters, i.e. with a data item having an editing character as part of its definition.

Having defined the format of the printlines, how can we output them to the printer?

First, we assign a file to the printer. We shall call this file PRINT-TABLE.

```
ENVIRONMENT DIVISION.
INPUT-OUTPUT SECTION.
FILE-CONTROL.
      SELECT PRINT-TABLE
           ASSIGN TO PRINTER.
```

Then we define PRINT-TABLE as

```
DATA DIVISION.
FILE SECTION.
FD  PRINT-TABLE
         LABEL RECORDS ARE OMITTED.
01  PRINTLINE  PIC X(80).
```

LABEL RECORDS ARE OMITTED because we are not dealing with a file on disk. The file PRINT-TABLE comprises the record defined by PRINTLINE. If you are using the Micro Focus (or a similar) COBOL compiler, or if several terminals share the same printer and the output to it is queued (i.e. spooled) you should consult the appendix.

To output the column-headings to the printer, we would code, in the PROCEDU-RE DIVISION, something like WRITE PRINTLINE FROM COLUMN-HEADINGS. And so to the algorithm.

```
write column-headings
write blank line
number ← 1
while (number <= 10) do
      square ← number x number
      cube ← number x square
      write report-line
      add 1 to number
endwhile
```

And the COBOL program.

```
* This program prints out a table of numbers,
* their squares and their cubes.

 IDENTIFICATION DIVISION.
 PROGRAM-ID.  TM61.

 ENVIRONMENT DIVISION.
 INPUT-OUTPUT SECTION.
 FILE-CONTROL.
     SELECT PRINT-TABLE
         ASSIGN TO PRINTER.

 DATA DIVISION.
 FILE SECTION.
 FD  PRINT-TABLE
         LABEL RECORDS ARE OMITTED.
 01  PRINTLINE  PIC X(80).
```

```
WORKING-STORAGE SECTION.
01  W1-COLUMN-HEADINGS.
      05   FILLER            PIC X(29)    VALUE SPACES.
      05   FILLER            PIC X(6)     VALUE "NUMBER".
      05   FILLER            PIC XX       VALUE SPACES.
      05   FILLER            PIC X(6)     VALUE "SQUARE".
      05   FILLER            PIC XXX      VALUE SPACES.
      05   FILLER            PIC X(4)     VALUE "CUBE".
      05   FILLER            PIC X(30)    VALUE SPACES.


01  W2-REPORT-LINE.
      05   FILLER            PIC X(31)    VALUE SPACES.
      05   W2-NUMBER-OUT     PIC Z9.
      05   FILLER            PIC X(5)     VALUE SPACES.
      05   W2-SQUARE-OUT     PIC ZZ9.
      05   FILLER            PIC X(5)     VALUE SPACES.
      05   W2-CUBE-OUT       PIC ZZZ9.
      05   FILLER            PIC X(30)    VALUE SPACES.


01  W3-NUMERIC-NON-EDITED-FIELDS.
      05   W3-NUMBER         PIC 99.
      05   W3-SQUARE         PIC 999.
      05   W3-CUBE           PIC 9999.


PROCEDURE DIVISION.
010-OPEN.
      OPEN OUTPUT PRINT-TABLE
      WRITE PRINTLINE FROM W1-COLUMN-HEADINGS
      MOVE   SPACES TO PRINTLINE
      WRITE PRINTLINE
      MOVE 1 TO W3-NUMBER
      PERFORM 020-CALCULATE UNTIL (W3-NUMBER > 10)
      GO TO 030-CLOSE.

020-CALCULATE.
      MULTIPLY W3-NUMBER BY W3-NUMBER GIVING W3-SQUARE
      MULTIPLY W3-NUMBER BY W3-SQUARE GIVING W3-CUBE
      MOVE W3-NUMBER TO W2-NUMBER-OUT
      MOVE W3-SQUARE TO W2-SQUARE-OUT
      MOVE W3-CUBE TO W2-CUBE-OUT
      WRITE PRINTLINE FROM W2-REPORT-LINE
      ADD 1 TO W3-NUMBER.

030-CLOSE.
      CLOSE PRINT-TABLE.
      STOP RUN.
```

Exercise 6.1

1 Design, write, test and document a program which will tabulate (tabulate means produce a table) the number of litres per gallon for each gallon from one to twenty inclusive, and the number of gallons per litre for every five litres from five to 100 litres inclusive. Take one gallon as equivalent to 4.546 litres, and give all values correct to one decimal place.

2 A common task in data processing is to use a computer to fill in the blanks in a pre-printed form, e.g. bank cheques. This means that the pre-printed stationery must be accurately aligned in the printer before the forms are filled in. Further, the forms are often continuous, i.e. each form is separated from the next by a line of perforations. A line-up routine is required which will enable the computer operator to align the forms correctly with the minimum of wastage.

Design and write a program which will enable an operator (or user) to align continuous stationery in the printer, according to the following specification.

while (not aligned-ok) do
        print two rectangles of asterisks, one directly below the other,
                each rectangle to be the size of a page.
        above the bottom line of the first rectangle write the message

IF PERFORATIONS DO NOT APPEAR BETWEEN TWO BOXES OF
ASTERISKS, RE-ALIGN PAPER AND REPRINT

        below the top line of the second rectangle repeat the message.
endwhile

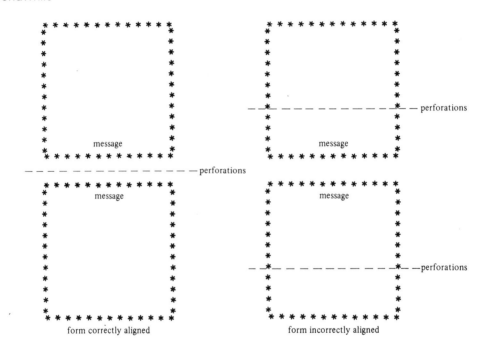

Each page is 11 inches long by 8.5 inches wide, (i.e. standard listing size, approximately A4).

6.3 PAGE FORMATS

Files are often interrogated to produce various printed reports. Suppose a report of all students who passed the C and G exam is to be produced from a computer file of exam results. What should the report look like? What should the report contain?

Names of successful candidates, together with their grades are certainly required. A page heading to indicate what the printout is concerned with would be useful, and, if there were many successful candidates, then several pages, and hence a page number and a heading on each page would be needed.

In general, a good report layout would include

a report heading stating the purpose of the report and the
    date on which the report was printed;
column headings on each page;
good spacing of columns across the page;
borders at top and bottom of each page;
a page number on each page.

Suppose the report is to be printed on pages measuring about 8.5 by 11 inches; this allows about 80 characters to be printed on each line, and about 66 lines on each page (six lines per inch).

Look at Figure 6.2. A top margin of seven clear lines is specified and fifty lines are to be printed in the body of the report on each page (this includes the headings).

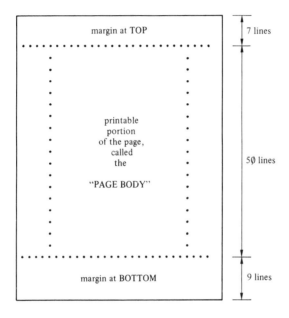

How can the number of lines to a page be specified? In COBOL, the total page size is defined in the LINAGE clause. For example

```
DATA DIVISION.
FILE SECTION.
FD  EXAM-RESULTS-REPORT
    LABEL RECORDS ARE OMITTED
    LINAGE IS 50 LINES
        LINES AT TOP 7
        LINES AT BOTTOM 9.
*  ( Total page size = 50 + 7 + 9 lines
*                    = 66 lines )
```

We now have some idea about what constitutes a page. How can we determine when the end of page has been reached? One way is to use the END–OF–PAGE clause provided in COBOL. Every time a line in the page body is printed, COBOL

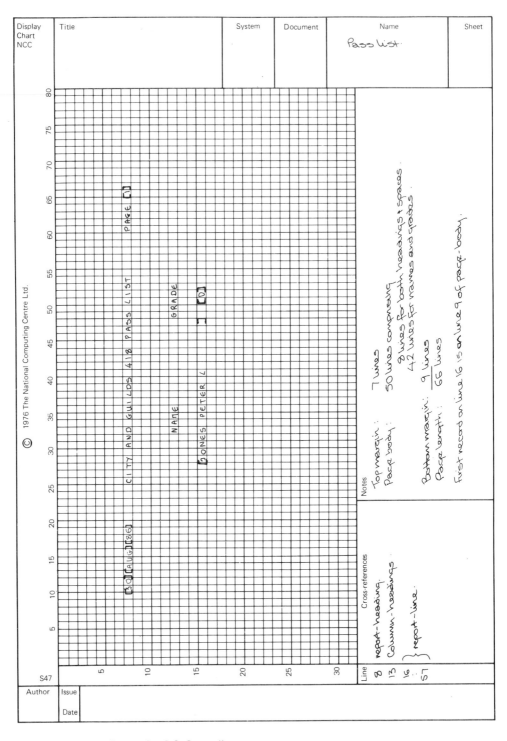

Figure 6.2   Printer format for C & G passlist

increments its own line–counter. When the value of this line-counter reaches the foot of the page body, for example, the END–OF–PAGE has been reached.

```
if (end–of–page = true) then
    move to next page
    write page headings
    write column headings
    add 1 to page–number
    reset line–number
    end–of–page ← false
endif
write results–record
add 1 to line–number
if (line–number > FOOT–OF–PAGE) then
  end–of–page ← true
endif
```

In COBOL we might write something like

```
IF  (W–END–OF–PAGE  =  "TRUE")
      WRITE PRINTLINE FROM REPORT–HEADING
          AFTER ADVANCING PAGE
      WRITE PRINTLINE FROM COLUMN–HEADINGS
          AFTER ADVANCING 5 LINES
      WRITE PRINTLINE FROM REPORT–LINE
          AFTER ADVANCING 3 LINES
      ADD 1 TO PAGE–COUNT
      MOVE "FALSE" TO W–END–OF–PAGE.
  WRITE PRINTLINE FROM REPORT–LINE
      AT END–OF–PAGE MOVE "TRUE" TO W–END–OF–PAGE.
```

The footing clause may be used to define the last line in the page body on which a record is to be printed.

```
LINEAGE IS 50 LINES
      WITH FOOTING AT 50
      LINES AT TOP 7
      LINES AT BOTTOM 9.
```

The LINAGE clause specifies the page size. So, when WRITE PRINTLINE FROM REPORT-HEADING AFTER ADVANCING PAGE is executed, nine blank lines at the bottom of the current page are printed and then seven blank lines at the top of the next page. So, the paper in the printer is automatically positioned at line eight — the correct position for the page heading.

We are now in a position to design a program for the following task.

A program is required which will produce the listing (i.e. report) showing all students who passed the C and G exam. Input to the program is the file of exam results, which contains names and grades. A grade is one from fail, refer, pass, credit or distinction. Only the grades pass, credit or distinction count as a pass.

There are several methods for designing the algorithm. Here is one of them. We start by outlining what needs to be done.

```
startup
while (not eof results-file) do { eof – end of file }
    write-and-read
endwhile
closedown
stop
```

Now, we add some more detail to startup, write-and-read and closedown.
In closedown, files are closed.

```
closedown
     close results-file, printer-file
```

In startup, files are opened, headings are printed on the first page, and the first record is retrieved from the results-file.

```
startup
     open printer–file for writing
     open results-file for reading
     page-number ← 1
     end–of–page ← true
     retrieve first results–record
     if (end–of–file = true) then
        display "Error-no records in results-file"
     endif
```

In write-and-read, if the candidate has passed, the record is written to the printer; the next record is retrieved from the results-file.

```
write-and-read
     if (end–of–page = true) then
        write headings
        add 1 to page-number
        reset line-number
        end–of–page ← false
     endif
     if (grade = distinction or credit or pass)
        write results-record
        add 1 to line-number
        if (line-number > FOOT-OF-PAGE) then
        end-of-page ← true
        endif
     endif
     retrieve next results-record
```

Now, we translate the structured English into COBOL.

```
startup
while (not eof results-file) do
     write and read
endwhile
closedown
stop
```

becomes

```
PROCEDURE DIVISION.
010-MAIN.
    PERFORM 020-STARTUP
    PERFORM 030-WRITE-AND-READ UNTIL W-EOF = "TRUE"
    PERFORM 040-CLOSEDOWN
    STOP RUN.
```

We have a hierarchy of modules or paragraphs. This hierarchy can be represented by the following diagram.

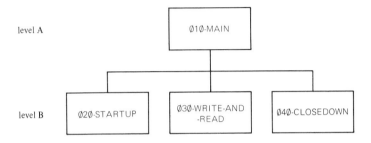

Paragraphs at level B are at a lower level than the paragraph at level A. In general, paragraphs at a lower level should contain more detail than paragraphs at a higher level. For example, 010-MAIN says execute 020-STARTUP, then 030-WRITE-AND-READ, then 040-CLOSE-DOWN, then stop; it represents a summary of what the program is doing. 020-STARTUP contains the details of how the files are opened, and how the first record is retrieved from the file.

startup and closedown are translated into COBOL as paragraphs BA-START-UP and BC-CLOSE-DOWN in program TM62.

Exercise 6.2

1(a) Enter and compile the following program, TM62.

1(b) Now amend the program by including the details for paragraph BB-WRITE-AND-READ.

1(c) Create the results file and test the program. (How many records should the results file contain in order to test whether the program can output more than one page of results correctly?)

1(d) Amend the program so that the grade is written out in full. For example, if a grade for a results-record is "D", then "distinction" (and not "D") is to be printed.

```
*  { This program prints a listing of students who passed the }
*  { City and Guilds Exam.                                     }

   IDENTIFICATION DIVISION.
   PROGRAM-ID.   TM62.

   ENVIRONMENT DIVISION.
   INPUT-OUTPUT SECTION.
   FILE-CONTROL.
        SELECT EXAM-RESULTS-REPORT ASSIGN TO PRINTER.
        SELECT F1-RESULTS-FILE ASSIGN TO DISK
               ORGANIZATION LINE SEQUENTIAL.
*        { ORGANIZATION is LINE SEQUENTIAL means that the file was
*          created by using a text editor.  In such a file, each
*          record is terminated with a carriage-return/line-feed
*          signal (obtained by pressing return), and each field is
*          padded out with spaces, if necessary, to the size specified
*          in the PICture statements. }
   DATA DIVISION.
   FILE SECTION.
   FD   EXAM-RESULTS-REPORT
        LABEL RECORDS OMITTED
        LINAGE IS 50 LINES
             WITH FOOTING AT 50
             LINES AT TOP 7
             LINES AT BOTTOM 9.
   01   PRINTLINE PIC X(80).

   FD   F1-RESULTS-FILE
        LABEL RECORDS STANDARD
        VALUE OF FILE-ID IS "B:CGRESULT.DAT".
   01   F1-RESULTS-RECORD.
        05 F1-NAME    PIC X(20).
        05 F1-GRADE   PIC X.
```

```
WORKING-STORAGE SECTION.
01    WA-REPORT-HEADING.
      05    FILLER                PIC X(10)    VALUE SPACES.
      05    WA-REPORT-DAY         PIC 99.
      05    FILLER                PIC X        VALUE SPACES.
      05    WA-REPORT-MONTH       PIC XXX.
      05    FILLER                PIC X        VALUE SPACES.
      05    WA-REPORT-YEAR        PIC 99.
      05    FILLER                PIC X(6)     VALUE SPACES.
      05    FILLER                PIC X(29)    VALUE
                                  "CITY AND GUILDS 418 PASS LIST".
      05    FILLER                PIC X(6)     VALUE SPACES.
      05    FILLER                PIC X(4)     VALUE "PAGE".
      05    FILLER                PIC X        VALUE SPACES.
      05    WA-REPORT-PAGE        PIC 99.
      05    FILLER                PIC X(13)    VALUE SPACES.

01    WB-REPORT-COLUMNS.
      05    FILLER                PIC X(32)    VALUE SPACES.
      05    FILLER                PIC X(4)     VALUE "name".
      05    FILLER                PIC X(12)    VALUE SPACES.
      05    FILLER                PIC X(5)     VALUE "grade".
      05    FILLER                PIC X(27)    VALUE SPACES.

01    WC-REPORT-LINE.
      05    FILLER                PIC X(28)    VALUE SPACES.
      05    WC-REPORT-NAME        PIC X(20).
      05    FILLER                PIC XX       VALUE SPACES.
      05    WC-REPORT-GRADE       PIC X.
      05    FILLER                PIC X(29)    VALUE SPACES.

01    WD-SUNDRY-VARIABLES.
      05    WD-EOF                PIC X(5).
      05    WD-EOP                PIC X(5).
*     { EOF - End Of File,  EOP - End Of Page }

PROCEDURE DIVISION.
AA-MAIN.
      PERFORM BA-START-UP
      PERFORM BB-WRITE-AND-READ UNTIL WD-EOF = "TRUE"
      PERFORM BC-CLOSE-DOWN
      STOP RUN.
```

```
BA-START-UP.
    DISPLAY "Printing exam results"
    DISPLAY "Today's date?"
    DISPLAY "day number"
    ACCEPT WA-REPORT-DAY
    DISPLAY "month name"
    ACCEPT WA-REPORT-MONTH
    DISPLAY "year number (last two digits)"
    ACCEPT WA-REPORT-YEAR
    OPEN OUTPUT EXAM-RESULTS-REPORT
    OPEN INPUT F1-RESULTS-FILE
    MOVE 1 TO WA-REPORT-PAGE
    MOVE "TRUE" TO WD-EOP
    MOVE "FALSE" TO WD-EOF
    READ F1-RESULTS-FILE AT END
        DISPLAY "No records found in CGRESULT.DAT"
        MOVE "TRUE" TO WD-EOF.

BB-WRITE-AND-READ.
*    { to be completed }

BC-CLOSE-DOWN.
    CLOSE F1-RESULTS-FILE
    CLOSE EXAM-RESULTS-REPORT.
```

7
Screen Formatting

7.1 INTRODUCTION

Programs communicate with their users via the keybord and screen. The information displayed on the screen determines how effectively the program is used. For example, if the user finds the display irritating in any way, the program may not be used at all. The interface between the program and its user — the screen display is the subject of this chapter. In it, we examine some of the facilities offered by some COBOL compilers for formatting (arranging) the display on a screen, and consider some of the principles of designing a screen format.

7.2 SCREEN HANDLING FACILITIES

We can imagine the screen to be divided into a grid comprising (usually) 24 rows and 80 columns. (Remember that columns are upright.) Thus, we can imagine 24 x 80 = 1920 rectangles or grid locations. Each location is just big enough to hold one keyboard character. The top left hand location on the screen is at row 1, column 1. The bottom right hand location on the screen is at row 24, column 80. This is shown on the screen format sheet (Figure 7.1).

In the first program, we remove the clutter from the screen, display the word CENTRE in (more or less) the centre, and the phrase BOTTOM RIGHT in the bottom right hand corner of the screen.

```
IDENTIFICATION DIVISION.
PROGRAM-ID.  TM71.
ENVIRONMENT DIVISION.
DATA DIVISION.
SCREEN SECTION.
01  S-TEST.
    05  BLANK SCREEN.
    05  LINE 12 COLUMN 37 VALUE "CENTRE".
    05  LINE 24 COLUMN 68 VALUE "BOTTOM RIGHT".
PROCEDURE DIVISION.
010.
    DISPLAY S-TEST
    STOP RUN.
```

The SCREEN SECTION is the last section in the DATA DIVISION. The screen display named S-TEST comprises a BLANK SCREEN, followed by the word CENTRE beginning at line 12 column 37, followed by the phrase BOTTOM RIGHT beginning at line 24 column 68.

The screen name is chosen by the programmer. In this example it is S-TEST.

Different COBOL compilers have different commands for formatting output on a screen. The examples in this chapter are written in Microsoft COBOL. Examples written in Micro Focus COBOL can be found in the appendix.

In the second program, we move the cursor to a location of our choice. Suppose we wish to display the prompt Name? on line 6 starting at column 20, and to accept the

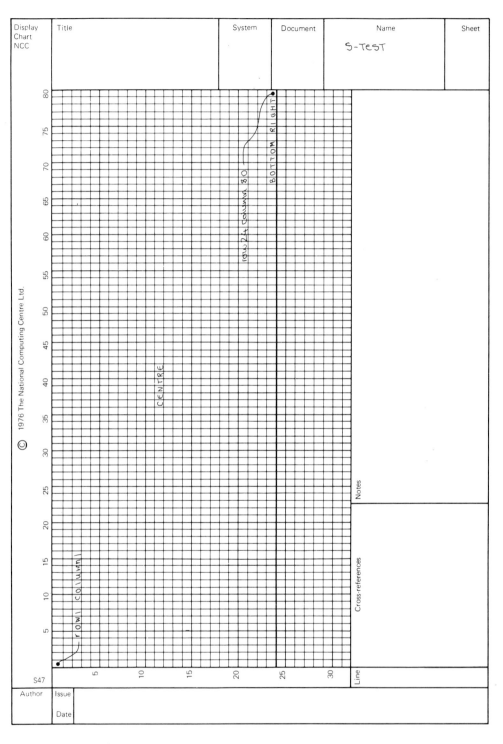

Figure 7.1   Screen format

reply, from the keyboard, so that what is entered appears on line 6 starting at column 28. We could code something like

```
DISPLAY (6, 20) "Name?"
ACCEPT (6, 28) W-NAME
```

Notice that a comma followed by a space separates a line number (e.g. 6) from a column number (e.g. 20).

```
IDENTIFICATION DIVISION.
PROGRAM-ID.  TM72.
ENVIRONMENT DIVISION.
DATA DIVISION.
WORKING-STORAGE SECTION.
01  W-NAME  PIC X(20).
SCREEN SECTION.
01  CLEAR-SCREEN.
    05  BLANK SCREEN.
PROCEDURE DIVISION.
010.
    DISPLAY CLEAR-SCREEN
    DISPLAY (6, 20) "Name?"
    ACCEPT (6, 28) W-NAME
    STOP RUN.
```

A limitation of writing something like

```
DISPLAY (6, 20) "Name?"
```

is that the coordinates (6, 20) are written into the program i.e. the coordinates cannot vary during program execution. Microsoft COBOL provides two numeric data items, LIN and COL, to represent LINe and COLumn numbers. The values of LIN and COL can be varied during program execution.

For example, suppose a seating plan for a small theatre is to be displayed on the screen — see Figure 7.2. One way of displaying a row of seats is

```
IDENTIFICATION DIVISION.
PROGRAM-ID.  TM73.
ENVIRONMENT DIVISION.
DATA DIVISION.
WORKING-STORAGE SECTION.
01  SEAT  PIC X(3)  VALUE "[ ]".

SCREEN SECTION.
01  SEAT-HEADING.
    05  BLANK SCREEN.
    05  LINE 6 COLUMN 29 VALUE "MAGIC THEATRE COMPANY".

PROCEDURE DIVISION.
010.
    DISPLAY SEAT-HEADING
    MOVE 8 TO LIN
    MOVE 27 TO COL
    PERFORM 020-PRINT-ROW UNTIL (COL > 53)
    GO TO 030.

020-PRINT-ROW.
    DISPLAY (LIN, COL) SEAT
    ADD 3 TO COL.

030.
    STOP RUN.
```

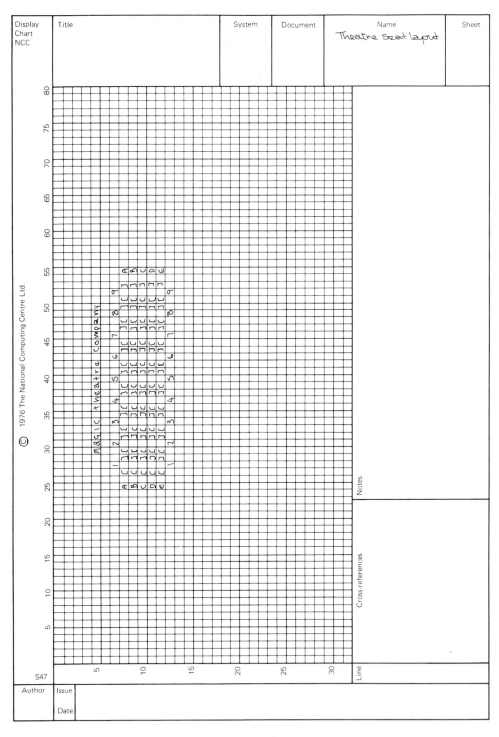

Figure 7.2   Screen format showing theatre seating plan

Notice that LIN and COL are not declared in WORKING-STORAGE — they are already provided. The values of LIN and COL can be increased or decreased by adding or subtracting an integer value. Also, integer values can be MOVEd to LIN or COL.

The program which displays all the seats in the seating plan requires just a little more thought. We need to display a seat at (lin, col) for whatever values lin and col have.

```
display (lin, col) seat
```

To display a line of seats, we need to hold the value of lin constant, and vary the value of col.

```
col ← 27
while (col <= 51)
        display (lin, col) seat
        add 3 to col { each seat takes up 3 columns on the screen }
endwhile
```

But we have several lines of seats.

```
for each line of seats
        col ← 27
        while (col <= 51)
                display (lin, col) seat
                add 3 to col
        endwhile
endfor
```

So, for each value of lin, we vary the value of col.

```
lin ← 8
while (lin <= 12)
        col ← 27
        while (col <= 51)
                display (lin, col) seat
                add 3 to col
        endwhile
        add 1 to lin
endwhile
```

When lin = 8, col ranges from 27 to 51, then lin becomes 9. When lin = 9, col ranges from 27 to 51, then lin becomes 10. When lin = 10, col ranges from 27 to 51, then lin becomes 11. This is repeated for lin = 11 and for lin = 12. Translating this into COBOL:

```
START.
    MOVE 8 TO LIN
    PERFORM PRINT-LINE UNTIL (LIN > 12)
    GO TO STOP.

PRINT-LINE.
    MOVE 27 TO COL
    PERFORM PRINT-SEAT UNTIL (COL > 51)
    ADD 1 TO LIN.
```

```
PRINT-SEAT.
    DISPLAY (LIN, COL) SEAT
    ADD 3 TO COL.

STOP.
```

Here is the complete program.

```
IDENTIFICATION DIVISION.
PROGRAM-ID. TM74.
ENVIRONMENT DIVISION.
DATA DIVISION.
WORKING-STORAGE SECTION.
01  SEAT  PIC X(3)  VALUE "[ ]".

SCREEN SECTION.
01  SEAT-HEADING.
    05  BLANK SCREEN.
    05  LINE 5 COLUMN 29 VALUE "MAGIC THEATRE COMPANY".

PROCEDURE DIVISION.
010-START.
    DISPLAY SEAT-HEADING
    MOVE 8 TO LIN
    PERFORM 020-PRINT-LINE UNTIL (LIN > 12)
    GO TO 040-STOP.

020-PRINT-LINE.
    MOVE 27 TO COL
    PERFORM 030-PRINT-SEAT UNTIL (COL > 51)
    ADD 1 TO LIN.

030-PRINT-SEAT.
    DISPLAY (LIN, COL) SEAT
    ADD 3 TO COL.

040-STOP.
    STOP RUN.
```

Exercise 7.1

1   Test programs TM71, TM72, TM73 and TM74 on your computer.

2   Modify program TM74 so that it displays the seat row letter and column number; use an array to hold the letters.

3   When access to a confidential file is protected by a password, the password should not appear on the screen. The following program prevents unauthorised people from reading the password off the screen.

```
IDENTIFICATION DIVISION.
PROGRAM-ID. TM75.
ENVIRONMENT DIVISION.
DATA DIVISION.
WORKING-STORAGE SECTION.
01  W-PASSWORD  PIC X(10).

SCREEN SECTION.
01  PASSWORD-SCREEN.
    05 BLANK SCREEN.
    05 LINE 10 COLUMN 30 VALUE "PASSWORD?  ".
    05 S-PASSWORD PIC X(10) SECURE TO W-PASSWORD.
```

```
PROCEDURE DIVISION.
010.
    DISPLAY PASSWORD-SCREEN.
    ACCEPT S-PASSWORD
    IF (W-PASSWORD = "TM")
        DISPLAY (12, 5) "ACCESS PERMISSION GRANTED"
    ELSE
        DISPLAY (12, 5) "PASSWORD NOT VALID".
    STOP RUN.
```

Write a program which will accept a password from the user and compare it with a set of valid passwords held in a file. Every password entered by a user should be logged i.e. appended to another file of passwords used. (To add a record onto the end of a file that already exists, use the phrase OPEN EXTEND instead of OPEN OUTPUT.) The user is allowed up to three attempts to enter a valid password. On a fourth attempt, the program should terminate with a suitable message.

4 ACCEPTing a character from the keyboard without the need to press carriage return is sometimes useful. In Microsoft COBOL, this is achieved by coding something like

```
ACCEPT (LIN, COL) CHOICE WITH AUTO-SKIP
```

Test the following program, TM76.

```
IDENTIFICATION DIVISION.
PROGRAM-ID.   TM76.
ENVIRONMENT DIVISION.
DATA DIVISION.
WORKING-STORAGE SECTION.
01  W-CHOICE  PIC X.
SCREEN SECTION.
01  MENU-SCREEN.
    05 BLANK SCREEN.
    05 LINE 2 COLUMN 1 VALUE "Menu: A(mend, I(nsert, D(elete:
PROCEDURE DIVISION.
010.
    DISPLAY MENU-SCREEN
    ACCEPT (2, 23) W-CHOICE WITH AUTO-SKIP
    IF (W-CHOICE = "A" OR "a")
        DISPLAY "Amend an existing record"
    ELSE IF (W-CHOICE = "I" OR "i")
        DISPLAY (5, 5) "Insert a new record"
    ELSE IF (W-CHOICE = "D" OR "d")
        DISPLAY (5, 5) "Delete an unwanted record"
    ELSE
        DISPLAY (5, 5) W-CHOICE " is not on the menu".
    STOP RUN.
```

7.3 PRINCIPLES OF SCREEN LAYOUT DESIGN

The screen layout is an important part of the interface between a program and its user. If the user finds the screen displays confusing or irritating, the program is likely to be used incorrectly or disliked.

A good screen layout is simple, clear and easy for the user to understand.

Who is the user? The user may be a computing expert (e.g. yourself!) or may not have used a computer before. The user may be an expert in their own field (e.g. an accountant) or may receive only minimal training. The user may use the computer daily (e.g. a holiday bookings clerk), or only occasionally (e.g. the organiser of the annual marathon). The user may initially know nothing about how to use a computer, but end up being an expert on using a particular program (e.g. a journalist with a word processor). The user's customers may affect the way in which the user works. For example, a doctor using a computerised medical records system deals with patients. Some patients will bring their personal identity number (which is used to identify and retrieve the patient's record from the computer file) with them to the surgery, and some will not. A doctor cannot turn patients away just because they have not got their personal identity number with them.

A particular style of screen display may be ideal for one type of user, but an insult to another. Therefore, when designing screen displays, the first requirement is to identify the user. The second requirement is to know how the user works and thinks, and what language i.e. the kind of words, is used by the user. For example, a doctor would use the world 'invalid' to mean a person who was ill; a lawyer might use the same word to mean having no legal force. In reality, you might have to work with the user for several months to learn the user's methods and language. The screen display should be designed with the user in mind as well as the use to which it will be put. Here are some guidelines to help you design a screen display.

The display should be simple. Avoid unnecessary use of underlining and elaborate displays. Do not use reverse video (dark writing on a bright background) — it is hard on the eyes. Use blinking or flashing text sparingly — perhaps to draw attention to a particular word in a mass of text. Use the terminal's buzzer only if you must — perhaps to draw attention to an error message which requires immediate attention. Flashing text is hard on the eyes. Beeps and buzzes are annoying. Fancy displays irritate serious users.

The display should be clear. Do not clutter a display with irrelevant detail. Consider using upper case for headings and prompts, and lower case for text and data. Use either right justified prompts or headings with left justified entries

```
        AGE:    23
 OCCUPATION:    programmer
```

or left justified headings with left justified entries

```
 AGE:           23
 OCCUPATION:    programmer
```

Remember to put two or three spaces between prompt or heading and response or data values.

```
 SURNAME?  Patel
```

Centre headings above columns. Spread columns out uniformly across the screen. Here, four spaces between columns and the entire width of the screen are used.

```
AT. NUMBER       DESCRIPTION        UNIT    QTY    UNIT PRICE    VALUE
   2476H         floppy disks ds/dd   10     3        23.50      70.50
   3936P         listing paper      2000     5        17.50      87.50
   1834E         printer ribbons       5     1        15.75      15.75
```

Text should be left justified, integers right justified, and real numbers aligned under the decimal point.

The display should be well balanced. Group and spread the screen entries out so that the blank spaces do not appear to be bunched more in one part of the screen than in another. Group related data items together. For example, if a screen displays information on a horse, its rider and owner, then the data about the horse should be grouped together in a block, the data about the rider should be in its own group, as should the data on the owner. To minimise clutter on the screen, use blank space to separate the groups, not lines of dots, dashes or symbols such as :. Indent under group headings. For example,

```
HORSE
    NAME:   Satisfaction            COLOUR:  brown     HEIGHT:  16.3
    SIRE:   Jumping Jack Flash         AGE:  9             SEX:  gelding


OWNER
    NAME:   W Weaver                NUMBER:  2746h


RIDER
    NAME:   C Whitehurst            NUMBER:  3719g     COLOURS:  black/g
```

Be consistent. Direct the user's attention around the screen in a natural way, from left to right, from top to bottom, or clockwise. Always place error messages in the same place — at the top of the screen, or immediately after erroneous input, for example. Surround error messages or warnings with a symbol such as ***. For example,

```
        *** WARNING - patient more than 100 years old ***
```
or
```
        *** ERROR - patient more than 150 years old ***
```

Be consistent in your use of auto-skip or RETURN for data entry. For example, a customer-surname field twelve characters wide will not always be completely filled. Thus, if

```
        ACCEPT (LIN, COL) CUST-SURNAME WITH AUTO-SKIP
```

was coded, most names that are input will be terminated by pressing RETURN, and some will be terminated as soon as twelve characters are entered. If each customer has a five-digit identity number, and if

```
        ACCEPT (LIN, COL) CUST-ID WITH AUTO-SKIP
```

was coded, then all customer-id's entered will be terminated as soon as the five characters are entered. To be consistent, either all data entry should be terminated with RETURN, or all data entry should be terminated automatically as soon as each field is filled. Inconsistent screen displays confuse users.

The display should be understandable to the user. Avoid abbreviations — use complete words wherever possible.

Do not leave the user wondering whether the computer is working. Respond immediately to every request made by the user, by displaying a message or a new screen, for example. If a process, such as searching, takes some time to complete, then display a message like

"searching for name . . . please wait".

Four types of screen display — data entry, enquiry, question and answer, and menu — are illustrated in the following examples.

TM HORSE TRIAL ENTRY FORM

BLOCK CAPITALS PLEASE.

Venue ....   Date ....

COMMUNICATIONS TO

    Name ....

    Address ....

    ....

    Post code ....   Tel ....

HORSE

    Name ....   Colour ....

    Sex ....   Height ....   Age ....   Reg. no. ....

    Sire ....

OWNER

    Name ....   Membership no. ....

RIDER

    Name ....   Membership no. ....

OTHER HORSES

    If competitor is riding several horses, please list them in the preferred order of riding.

        1. ....

        2. ....

        3. ....

REQUESTS

    If you wish to start in the afternoon, please tick ☐

    If you require overnight stabling, please tick ☐

    Other requests ....

Signed ....   Date ....

7.3.1 DATA ENTRY

Data entry screens are often used for entering data into a computer file. If the data already exists on a form, then the data entry screen should look like the form. For example, on the next page is a form which is filled in by people who wish to enter their horse in a competition.

The competitions, called horse trials, are held at various locations throughout the summer. At each location, there is a horse trials organiser. Competitors send completed forms to the organiser of their choice. Each organiser transfers the information from the completed form into the computer.

Figure 7.3 shows the corresponding screen format. Compressing an A4 sized form into a screen measuring 24 rows by 80 columns sometimes causes problems. In our example, we have just managed to squeeze it in. Sometimes, two or more screens, called pages, will be required.

The screen name and page number are shown in the top right hand corner. The overall layout of the screen is just like the form. The main headings are in capitals. There are at least two spaces after a sub-heading or prompt. The spaces allowed for the user to input the data are called input fields. The extent of input fields are marked x————x on the screen format sheet. The lengths of input fields are not shown on the screen. There are four spaces between the end of an input field and the next sub-heading or prompt. Column 80 is not used, because, on some terminals, a character entered in column 80 creates a carriage-return-line-feed signal, causing the cursor to move to the next line down. Similar problems might occur on line 24. There is a block of blank space in the bottom right hand corner of the screen layout, giving it a slightly unbalanced appearance. On the other hand, the screen layout conforms quite closely to the form design.

If there is no input form, then the user should be asked to help with the design of the data entry screen: the user knows the order in which the data for input is received.

7.3.2 ENQUIRY

Enquiry screens are used to display the contents of computer files in response to some request such as 'list the horses requiring overnight stabling'.

Only the contents of relevant fields should be shown, and the screen should be organised so that the user can quickly find the information required. For example, in the enquiry screen shown in Figure 7.4, the user looks from left to right to find the appropriate field, then looks down the column to find the required item.

The places at which horses are stabled overnight are local and known to the organiser; further details are not required. A blank space in the stabled at column shows that overnight stabling for the horse still needs to be arranged. If the organiser wishes to contact a person whose horse requires stabling, perhaps to inform them where to take their horse on arrival at the event, then another enquiry screen will show the person's name, address and phone number — see Figure 7.5.

Several people might have the same name. One person might enter more than one horse. The organiser selects the right person by looking for the horse's name. (No two horses have the same name.) Again, only the relevant information is shown.

7.3.3 QUESTION AND ANSWER

Question and answer screens are used to guide the user through some process, such as backing up (i.e. making a copy of) data files. The screen comprises a sequence of questions, produced by the program, and answers input by the user — see Figure 7.6.

The top line is reserved for error messages such as "cannot find competitors' file". The menu path (top right hand corner), the heading, the explanation of what the

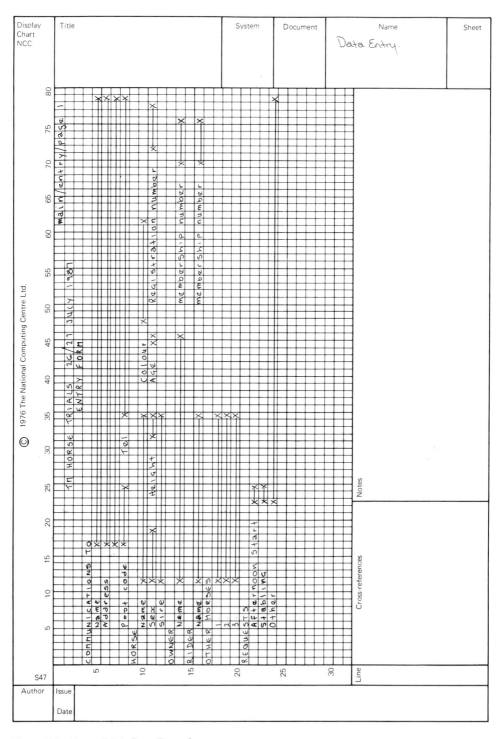

Figure 7.3 Horse Trials Data Entry Screen

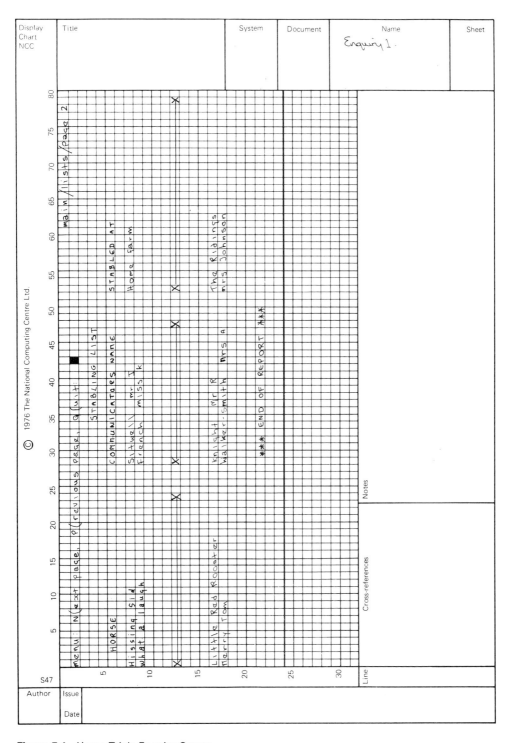

Figure 7.4 Horse Trials Enquiry Screen

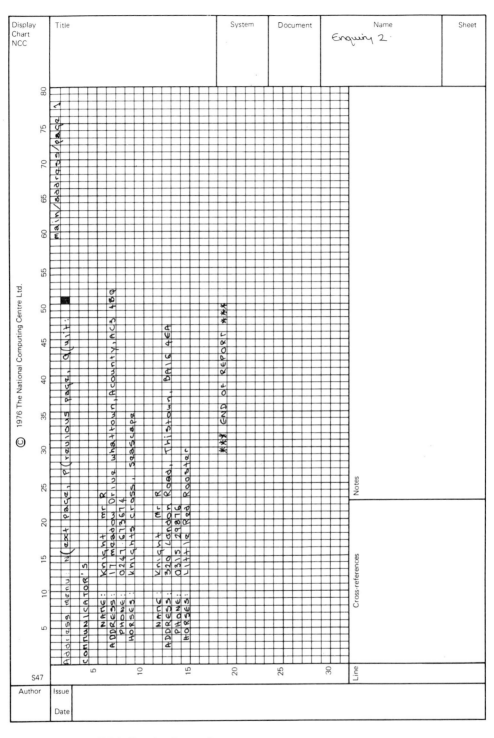

Figure 7.5   Horse Trials Enquiry Screen 2

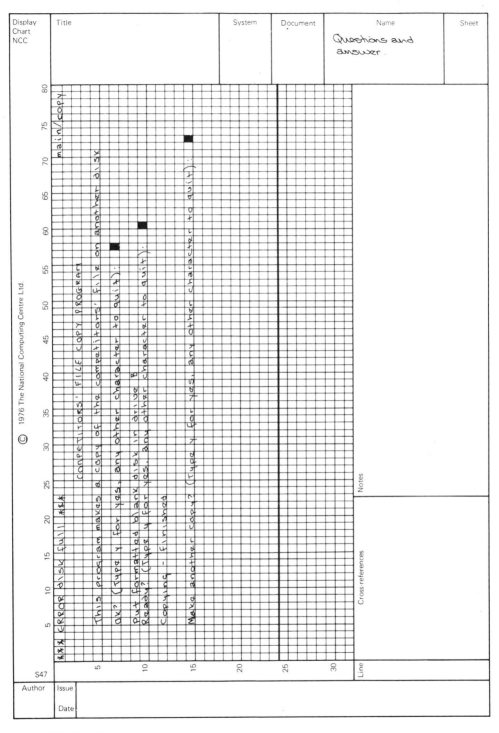

Figure 7.6 Question and answer screen

program does, and the first question is displayed. Then the user enters a character. If the character is not a y or a Y, then the question and answer screen is quitted; if the character is a y or a Y, the next instruction ("Put formatted blank disk in drive B") and question ("Ready? (Type y for yes, any other character to quit)") appears on the screen. The user then keys in a response. If y or Y is entered, the message, "copying —" is immediately displayed. When the copying has finished, the message "finished" comes up on the screen, and the user is given the opportunity of making another copy or quitting.

7.3.4 MENU

A menu lists the items that a user can choose — just like the menu in a cafe — see Figure 7.7. The menu is positioned in the middle of the screen. The heading is displayed in block capitals. The items on the menu are listed, left justified, in a column to help the user locate a particular item. The items are listed in order: the most frequently used item at the top of the list, and the least used item at the bottom. There are no more than eight items in the menu. Each item is numbered, starting with 1. There are three spaces between the full stop following the number and the item to which it refers. The prompt (Choice?) is separated from the menu and is displayed in line with the numbers.

Perhaps a better prompt would be Number? to indicate that the number corresponding to the user's choice should be entered. A prompt such as "Please enter the number corresponding to your choice:" is not used because it contains more words than are necessary, especially after the user has seen the program working.

The language used in the list of items is English and not computing jargon. For example, Bring entries file up to date is used insted of Update entries file (although the word update is now becoming part of everyday vocabulary). And View entry information is used rather than interrogate entries file.

When the user enters the number 1, for example, the file update menu is immediately shown — see Figure 7.8. The menu path is displayed (top right hand corner) to show the current position in the hierarchy of menus. If the user now enters 3, for example, the menu path displayed on the delete menu will be main/update/ delete. No more than three levels of menu are used.

Inexperienced users find detailed menus reassuring and helpful, but experienced users can find such menus tedious. Inexperienced users often become experienced users. A reasonable compromise might be to put the menu on one line. For example,

Main: U(pdate, V(iew, P(rint, A(ssign, K(opy, N(ew, C(hange, Q(uit: x

The name of the menu, Main, is followed by a colon, and the possible options. A colon follows the last item. There are two clear spaces between the last colon and the position where the user makes a selection. The user enters an upper case letter (U, V, P, . . . or Q) to select a choice. This menu is harder to understand and learn than a more detailed one because the beginner would need to remember details about each option. For example, the user would need to remember that N(ew means "create a new entries file". On the other hand, the menu may be a sufficient reminder to the experienced user. The computing term update is used instead of amend because A(mend would clash with A(ssign, (A selects both of them) and another menu uses A(mend to mean amend a record. If a choice is selected with auto-skip, then movement around a menu system can be quick enough to satisfy the experienced user. This is a good case for using auto-skip.

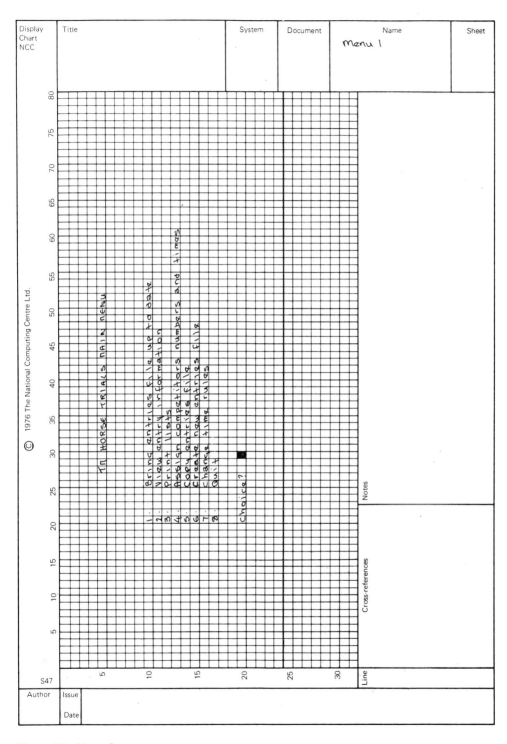

Figure 7.7 Menu Screen

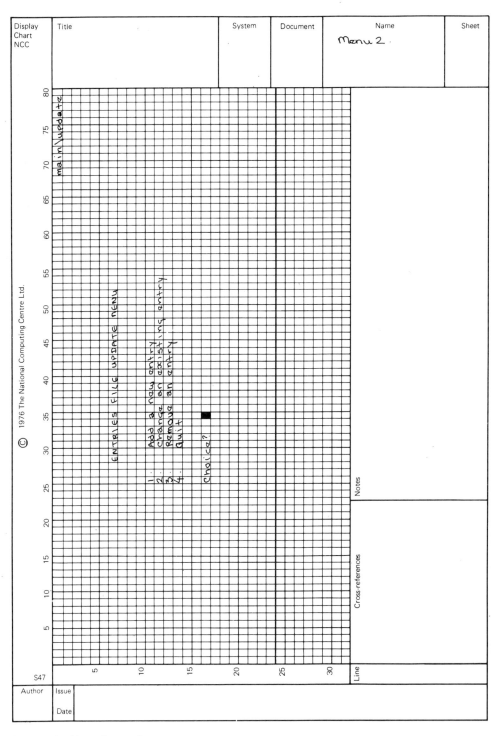

Figure 7.8 Menu Screen 2

Exercise 7.2

1 Design the dialogue (screen displays) for a program which is to be used by the local constabulary. The program is to maintain a register (i.e. a file) of bicycles and their owners.

A bicycle usually has a unique number stamped on its frame by its manufacturer. When a person presents a bicycle for registration by the police, its frame number (if it has one) or the postcode and house number (if the frame has previously been registered) is entered and the file searched. If the bicycle has already been registered and the person is not the registered owner, the constabulary establish whether the person is the legal owner. If the bicycle has never been registered, or is to be re-registered, the person's name and address is entered and the file updated. The owner's postcode and house number is stamped on the frame by the constabulary.

The constabulary should be able to view the contents of the register in surname order, in street-name order, and in postcode-with-house-number order.

Implement your design in COBOL. You do not need to update the file or sort it — the purpose of this exercise is screen design.

8

Indexed Files

8.1 INTRODUCTION

In the chapter on serial files (Chapter 5) we examined some of the properties of serial file organisation. A distinguishing feature of serial file organisation is that records are accessed in the same order in which they were written onto the storage medium. A consequence of this is that it can take some time to access and retrieve information from, say, the 1000th record in sequence because each of the previous 999 records would have to be read into memory and examined. The time taken to access a particular record can be reduced if an index together with a means of directly locating the position of the record is used.

8.2 INDEXED FILES

For example, suppose a file of motor vehicle registration numbers and their owners has the following structure.

```
motor-vehicle-file
    vehicle-record
        registration-number              key
        registered-owner
            name
            address
```

Each record is uniquely identified by the value held in its registration-number field. This means that no two values for registration-number are identical. Hence, registration-number is known as the *key field*. The key field forms part of the index. In COBOL, the index is organised and managed by the compiler, and, in Microsoft COBOL, this file is given the suffice KEY. We need not concern ourselves with the structure of the index.

To code an indexed file data structure in COBOL, the file organisation is declared in the ENVIRONMENT DIVISION. Then the file structure is defined in the DATA DIVISION.

```
ENVIRONMENT DIVISION.
INPUT-OUTPUT SECTION.
FILE-CONTROL.
    SELECT F1-MOTOR-VEHICLE-FILE
        ASSIGN TO DISK
        ORGANIZATION IS INDEXED
        ACCESS MODE IS RANDOM
        RECORD KEY IS F1-REGISTRATION-NUMBER.
```

Notice the letter Z in ORGANIZATION. ACCESS MODE IS RANDOM means that a particular record can be accessed directly, i.e. without having to access all the previous records. The RECORD KEY clause declares that F1-REGISTRATION-NUMBER is the key field.

The file is declared in the DATA DIVISION as usual.

```
DATA DIVISION.
FILE SECTION.
FD  F1-MOTOR-VEHICLE-FILE
    LABEL RECORDS ARE STANDARD
    VALUE OF FILE-ID IS "A:VEHCL.DAT".
01  F1-VEHICLE.
    02  F1-REGISTRATION-NUMBER  PIC X(7).
    02  F1-REGISTERED-OWNER     PIC X(60).
```

Assuming the file to be already created, we now see how a particular record can be retrieved.

```
retrieve-a-record
    open motor-vehicle-file for reading in
    input registration-number from keyboard { load the key field }
    search index for registration-number
    if (registration-number is-not-in-index) then
        output "record for registration-number does not exist"
    otherwise
        retrieve vehicle-record { for registration-number }
        output vehicle-owner
    endif
    close motor-vehicle-file
```

One way of writing this algorithm in COBOL is

```
PROCEDURE DIVISION.
010-OPEN.
    OPEN INPUT F1-MOTOR-VEHICLE-FILE
    PERFORM 020-LOAD-AND-RETRIEVE
    GO TO 030-CLOSE.

020-LOAD-AND-RETRIEVE.
    DISPLAY "Motor vehicle number?"
    ACCEPT F1-REGISTRATION-NUMBER
    READ F1-MOTOR-VEHICLE-FILE RECORD
        INVALID KEY
            DISPLAY F1-REGISTRATION-NUMBER " is not on file'
            GO TO 030-CLOSE.
    DISPLAY F1-REGISTERED-OWNER.

030-CLOSE.
    CLOSE F1-MOTOR-VEHICLE-FILE
    STOP RUN.
```

With this algorithm, a single attempt to retrieve one record is made before halting. This is not very practical. In practice, the user is allowed to request a record retrieval as many times as required. The file remains open until the user has finished. Notice that the file is opened before the key field is given its value. Notice also the READ filename RECORD syntax: the word RECORD is compulsory.

The construction READ filename INVALID KEY do . . . . looks similar to READ filename AT END do . . . . . It means

examine the key value held in F1-REGISTRATION-NUMBER
if (it cannot be found in the KEY file) then
    execute the statements following the INVALID KEY clause
    { these statements are terminated by a full stop }
otherwise if (it can be found) then
    locate the corresponding record in F1-MOTOR-VEHICLE-FILE
    put a copy of this record into memory
endif

The key is checked for validity before a **READ** is executed.

Now we look at how the motor-vehicle-file can be created. The organisation and structure of the file is defined in exactly the same way as for record retrieval. The PROCEDURE DIVISION coding is

```
PROCEDURE DIVISION.
010-OPEN.
    OPEN OUTPUT F1-MOTOR-VEHICLE-FILE
    DISPLAY "Vehicle file creation - terminated by ***."
    DISPLAY "Vehicle registration number?"
    ACCEPT F1-REGISTRATION-NUMBER
    PERFORM 020-WRITE UNTIL (F1-REGISTRATION-NUMBER = "***")
    GO TO 030-CLOSE.

020-WRITE.
    DISPLAY "Name and address?
    ACCEPT F1-REGISTERED-OWNER
    WRITE F1-VEHICLE
        INVALID KEY
            DISPLAY "Cannot create record"
            DISPLAY F1-REGISTRATION-NUMBER " already exists.".

    DISPLAY "Vehicle registration number?"
    ACCEPT F1-REGISTRATION-NUMBER.

030-CLOSE.
    CLOSE F1-MOTOR-VEHICLE-FILE
    STOP RUN.
```

The construction **WRITE filename INVALID KEY do . . . .** means

examine the key value held in F1-REGISTRATION-NUMBER
if (it can be found in the KEY file) then
    execute the statements following the INVALID KEY clause
    { these statements are terminated by a full stop }
otherwise if (it cannot be found) then
    put a copy of the corresponding record { held in memory }
        onto the file { F1-MOTOR-VEHICLE-FILE }
    update the KEY file
endif

An important limitation is that no two records are allowed to have the same key value. If an attempt is made to create a record with a registration-number that already exists in the file, then the INVALID KEY clause is exercised. This can be a nuisance if, for example, you wish to index a file on surname. How this might be done is suggested in the chapter on linked lists and binary trees – Chapter 11.

Exercise 8.1

1 Design, write, test and document COBOL programs which will
(a) create an indexed file of about ten motor vehicle records. A record in this file should have the format

registration number   { this is the key field }
vehicle-type   { car, van or motorcycle }
vehicle-name-and-colour { make and model name }
owner-name-and-address

(b) retrieve from this indexed file the name and address of the owner together with vehicle details of any given vehicle registration number. If the record is not on the file, then a suitable message should be displayed.

8.3 INDEXED FILE UPDATE

A file of registered motor vehicles will not remain the same for long. When vehicles are scrapped, records are transferred to a scrapped-vehicles-file and deleted from the motor-vehicle-file. A record is created when a new vehicle is sold to its first owner. When a vehicle's owner changes, the record is amended.

The central part of an indexed file update algorithm is

```
while (not finished) do
        input-key { load the key field with a registration-number }
        search the motor-vehicle-file for the corresponding record
endwhile
```

input-key and search are underlined to show that these procedures are expanded in more detail and shown elsewhere. We expand on input-key and search next.

```
        input-key
                write out user instructions
                input registration-number

        search
                search index for registration-number
                if (registration-number is-not-in-index) then
                        { record for registration-number does not exist }
                        new-record
                otherwise
                        retrieve vehicle-record { for registration-number }
                        output vehicle-record
                        delete-or-amend
                endif
```

Now, new-record and delete-or-amend are detailed.

```
        new-record
                input rest of vehicle-record
                write vehicle-record to file
```

```
        delete-or-amend
            input update-type
            if (update-type = d) then
                delete vehicle-record from file
            else if (update-type = a)
                amend-the-record
            endif
```

And so on.

Now, how should the motor-vehicle-file be opened? In COBOL, a statement like

```
OPEN I-O F1-MOTOR-VEHICLE-FILE
```

allows a record to be accessed by the READ statement, modified, and then written back to the file to replace the original record.

The update algorithm introduces two more COBOL statements. To delete a record, DELETE F1-MOTOR-VEHICLE-FILE RECORD is coded. To write an amended record to the file, REWRITE F1-VEHICLE is coded.

Deferring details to a later stage is easily implemented. For example,

```
        while (not finished) do
            input-key
            search
        endwhile
```

could be written in COBOL as

```
010-CONTROL.
    MOVE "N" TO W-FINISHED
    PERFORM 020-LOOP UNTIL (W-FINISHED = "Y" OR "y")
    STOP RUN.

020-LOOP.
    PERFORM 030-INPUT-KEY
    PERFORM 040-SEARCH
    DISPLAY "Finished (y/n)?"
    ACCEPT W-FINISHED.
```

Then the details in paragraphs 030-INPUT-KEY and 040-SEARCH can be coded. This idea is explored further in the next exercise.

Exercise 8.2

1 The following (incomplete) COBOL program implements the update algorithm described above. Design and write an algorithm which will amend the fields of a vehicle-record held in memory and update the file. (The amendments are to be chosen by the program user.) Then incorporate your algorithm in the COBOL program. Test and document the completed program.

Making changes to a program written by someone else is a common activity in commercial data processing. This activity is often called program enhancement or maintenance. Programs are usually enhanced to meet changing requirements. A good maintenance programmer is able to make the changes in the same programming style as used by the original programmer (or programmers). The joins where the new coding is inserted cannot be detected.

```
* This program updates the motor-vehicle file.

 IDENTIFICATION DIVISION.
 PROGRAM-ID.   TM81.

 ENVIRONMENT DIVISION.
 INPUT-OUTPUT SECTION.
 FILE-CONTROL.
     SELECT F1-MOTOR-VEHICLE-FILE
         ASSIGN TO DISK
         ORGANIZATION IS INDEXED
         ACCESS MODE IS RANDOM
         RECORD KEY IS F1-REGISTRATION-NUMBER.

 DATA DIVISION.
 FILE SECTION.
 FD  F1-MOTOR-VEHICLE-FILE
     LABEL RECORDS ARE STANDARD
     VALUE OF FILE-ID IS "A:VEHCL.DAT".
 01  F1-VEHICLE.
     02  F1-REGISTRATION-NUMBER  PIC X(7).
     02  F1-MAKE-AND-COLOUR      PIC X(20).
     02  F1-REGISTERED-OWNER     PIC X(60).

 WORKING-STORAGE SECTION.
 01  W-FINISHED      PIC X.
 01  W-KEY-IS-FOUND  PIX X(5).
 01  W-UPDATE-TYPE   PIC X.

 PROCEDURE DIVISION.
 A-CONTROL SECTION.
 A10-CONTROL.
     OPEN I-O F1-MOTOR-VEHICLE-FILE
     MOVE "N" TO W-FINISHED
     PERFORM A20-LOOP UNTIL (W-FINISHED = "Y" OR "y")
     CLOSE F1-MOTOR-VEHICLE-FILE
     STOP RUN.

 A20-LOOP.
     PERFORM BA-INPUT-KEY
     PERFORM BB-SEARCH
     DISPLAY "Finished (y/n)?"
     ACCEPT W-FINISHED.

 BA-INPUT-KEY SECTION.
 BA10-INPUT-KEY.
     DISPLAY "Vehicle registration number?"
     ACCEPT F1-REGISTRATION-NUMBER.

 BB-SEARCH SECTION.
 BB10-SEARCH.
     MOVE "TRUE" TO W-KEY-IS-FOUND
     READ F1-MOTOR-VEHICLE-FILE RECORD
         INVALID KEY
             MOVE  "FALSE" TO W-KEY-IS-FOUND.
     IF (W-KEY-IS-FOUND = "TRUE")
         PERFORM CA-DELETE-OR-AMEND
     ELSE IF (W-KEY-IS-FOUND = "FALSE")
         PERFORM CB-NEW-RECORD.
```

```
CA-DELETE-OR-AMEND SECTION.
CA10-DELETE-OR-AMEND.
    DISPLAY F1-MAKE-AND-COLOUR
    DISPLAY F1-REGISTERED-OWNER
    DISPLAY "Enter d to delete this record"
    DISPLAY "      a to amend this record"
    DISPLAY "      n for neither delete nor amend"
    ACCEPT W-UPDATE-TYPE
    IF (W-UPDATE-TYPE = "d" OR "D")
        DELETE F1-MOTOR-VEHICLE-FILE RECORD
    ELSE IF (W-UPDATE-TYPE = "a" OR "A")
        PERFORM DA-AMEND.

CB-NEW-RECORD SECTION.
CB10-NEW-RECORD.
    DISPLAY "New vehicle"
    DISPLAY "Make and colour?"
    ACCEPT F1-MAKE-AND-COLOUR
    DISPLAY "Owner name and address?"
    ACCEPT F1-REGISTERED-OWNER
    WRITE F1-VEHICLE
        INVALID KEY
            DISPLAY "CB-NEW-RECORD - this should not happen".

DA-AMEND SECTION.
DA10-COMMENT.
* This is the section for you to design, write and test.
* The user amends any chosen field - except the registration-
* number field.  The amended record is then REWRITEn.
```

The **PROCEDURE DIVISION** is written in SECTIONs. Each SECTION has one or more paragraphs. The SECTIONs are organised in a hierarchical manner. The following diagram illustrates this hierarchy.

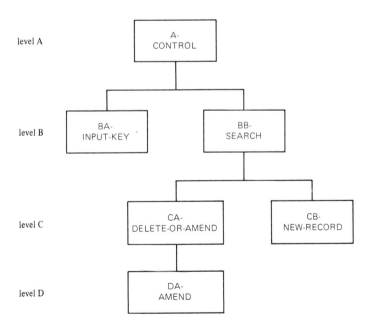

Figure 8.1   The hierarchical organisation of the sections in the COBOL program of Exercise 8.2

SECTION CB-NEW-RECORD is PERFORMed or executed from BB-SEARCH, i.e. control is passed from BB-SEARCH to CB-NEW-RECORD. After the statements in CB-NEW-RECORD have been executed, control is returned to BB-SEARCH. Hierarchical charts say nothing about the logic involved.

8.4 FILE MAINTENANCE

When a record is DELETEd, it is not physically removed from the file, but a flag is set to indicate that the record cannot be accessed: the record is logically deleted, not physically deleted. If many records are deleted, then the time taken to access a particular record may be longer than necessary. This is rectified by creating a new file, from the original, without the deleted records. This is achieved by copying the old file sequentially to the new one, as shown in the following program.

```
* This program creates a new motor-vehicle-file, from the
* original, without the deletions.

  IDENTIFICATION DIVISION.
  PROGRAM-ID.   TM82.
  ENVIRONMENT DIVISION.
  INPUT-OUTPUT SECTION.
  FILE-CONTROL.
      SELECT F1-MOTOR-VEHICLE-FILE
*             { this is the original motor-vehicle-file }
              ASSIGN TO DISK
              ORGANIZATION IS INDEXED
              ACCESS-MODE IS SEQUENTIAL
*             { in order to retrieve the records in key order }
              RECORD KEY IS F1-REGISTRATION-NUMBER.

      SELECT F2-MOTOR-VEHICLE-FILE
*             { this is the new, reformed motor-vehicle-file }
              ASSIGN TO DISK
              ORGANIZATION IS INDEXED
              ACCESS MODE IS SEQUENTIAL
              RECORD KEY IS F2-REGISTRATION-NUMBER.

  DATA DIVISION.
  FILE SECTION.

  FD  F1-MOTOR-VEHICLE-FILE
      LABEL RECORDS ARE STANDARD
      VALUE OF FILE-ID IS "A:VEHCL.DAT".
  01  F1-VEHICLE.
      02  F1-REGISTRATION-NUMBER  PIC X(7).
      02  FILLER                  PIC X(80).
*     { filler represents make, colour and registered owner }

  FD  F2-MOTOR-VEHICLE-FILE
      LABEL RECORDS ARE STANDARD
      VALUE OF FILE-ID IS "A:NEWVEHCL.DAT".
  01  F2-VEHICLE.
      02  F2-REGISTRATION-NUMBER  PIC X(7).
      02  FILLER                  PIC X(80).

  WORKING-STORAGE SECTION.
  01  W-EOF  PIC X(5).
```

```
PROCEDURE DIVISION.
010-CONTROL.
     OPEN INPUT F1-MOTOR-VEHICLE-FILE
     OPEN OUTPUT F2-MOTOR-VEHICLE-FILE
     MOVE "FALSE" TO W-EOF
     MOVE LOW-VALUE TO F1-REGISTRATION-NUMBER
     START F1-MOTOR-VEHICLE-FILE
          KEY GREATER THAN F1-REGISTRATION-NUMBER
*    { starts the sequential read from the first i.e. lowest
*     key value }
     READ F1-MOTOR-VEHICLE-FILE NEXT RECORD
          AT END MOVE "TRUE" TO W-EOF.
     PERFORM 020-LOOP UNTIL (W-EOF = "TRUE")
     CLOSE F1-MOTOR-VEHICLE-FILE
     CLOSE F2-MOTOR-VEHICLE-FILE
     DISPLAY "End of file re-construction"
     STOP RUN.

020-LOOP.
     WRITE F2-VEHICLE FROM F1-VEHICLE
          INVALID KEY
               DISPLAY "write error - this should not happen"
               MOVE "TRUE" TO W-EOF.

     READ F1-MOTOR-VEHICLE-FILE NEXT RECORD
          AT END MOVE "TRUE" TO W-EOF.
```

We end up with two files — the original one named VEHCL.DAT and the one we want to use in subsequent transactions, NEWVEHCL.DAT. If the first file was renamed as VEHCL.HIS, for example, (HIS for history) and then the latter file was renamed as VEHCL.DAT, the new file can be accessed by the original file amendment program. Many operating systems and COBOL compilers have a facility for renaming files. Here is a program, written in Microsoft COBOL, to do just that.

```
*  { This program renames files. }

   IDENTIFICATION DIVISION.
   PROGRAM-ID.   TM83.

   ENVIRONMENT DIVISION.

   DATA DIVISION.
   WORKING-STORAGE SECTION.
   01   W-OLDNAME        PIC X(14).
   01   W-NEWNAME        PIC X(14).
   01   W-ERROR-REPORT   PIC XX.

   PROCEDURE DIVISION.
   010-RENAME-FILES.
        MOVE "B:VEHCL.DAT" TO W-OLDNAME
        MOVE "B:VEHCL.HIS" TO W-NEWNAME
        PERFORM 020-RENAME
        MOVE "B:NEWVEHCL.DAT" TO W-OLDNAME
        MOVE "B:VEHCL.DAT" TO W-NEWNAME
        PERFORM 020-RENAME
        STOP RUN.

   020-RENAME.
        CALL 'RENAM' USING
             W-ERROR-REPORT, W-OLDNAME, W-NEWNAME
*            { Renames oldname as newname                          }
*            { Error report values are returned by the RENAM }
*            { function.                                          }
        IF (W-ERROR-REPORT = "00")
             DISPLAY W-OLDNAME " renamed successfully"
        ELSE IF (W-ERROR-REPORT = "30")
             DISPLAY W-OLDNAME " not found"
        ELSE IF (W-ERROR-REPORT = "40")
             DISPLAY "Syntax error in file name"
             STOP RUN.
```

8.5 INDEXED SEQUENTIAL FILES

Many small COBOL compilers, which are implemented on microcomputers, do not support true indexed sequential file organisation. But an indexed file together with a sequential read facility constitutes a file which is functionally equivalent to an indexed sequential file. So, for example, indexed files in Microsoft COBOL can be regarded as if they were indexed sequential files.

9
Sequential Files

9.1 INTRODUCTION

Every month, the personnel file in a large firm is updated; records for new employees are inserted, former employees' records are deleted, and records are amended when, for example, an employee moves from one department to another. Part of the record description might be

```
employee-record
      employee-number field          { this is the key field }
      employee-name field
      department field
```

The file is organised in ascending employee-number order. No two employees have the same employee-number. So, the value of employee-number uniquely identifies the employee-record. Consequently, the field employee-number is referred to as the key field.

A file in which the records are held in consecutive positions on the storage medium is known as a serial file. With a serial file, records are accessed in the same order in which they were written to the storage medium. If the records are held in key field order, then the file is also known as a sequential file. The file of employee records is an example of a sequential file because the records are held and accessed in employee-number order. Part of this file might look like

number	name	department
2476	HARRISON JM	DATA PROC
2477	KNOWLES D	PRODUCTION
2482	WATTS FG	DATA PROC
2483	GREEN P	ACCOUNTS
2490	CHAPMAN GR	SALES
2497	PARKER T	SALES

Suppose the amendments to the personnel-file are also held in a file, and this file is also organised sequentially. We shall call this file of amendments the transaction-file. A sequence of entries in this transaction-file might be

number	update-type	name	department
2476	A	HARRISON JM	SALES
2477	D		
2481	I	BAKER M	DATA PROC
2490	D		

where update-type A refers to an amendment e.g. a change of department, D signifies a record to be deleted, and update-type I indicates a record to be inserted. No other data values for update-type are allowed.

How can this transaction-file be used to update the personnel-file? One method is to 'merge' the personnel-file with the transaction-file to produce a new, updated personnel-file (Figure 9.1). We shall sometimes refer to the personnel-file as the personnel-master-file.

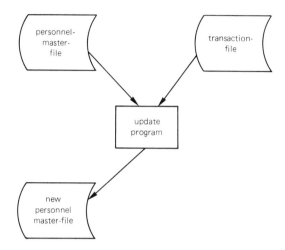

Figure 9.1   Outline of master file update process.

9.2 SEQUENTIAL FILE UPDATE

In order to concentrate on the algorithm for updating the personnel-file, we shall restrict the records to one field only — the key field. We shall refer to the (original) personnel-file as the master-file, and the new updated personnel-file as the new-file. Record names of M, T and N refer to the master-file, transaction-file and new-file respectively.

When the master-file is merged with the transaction-file, we expect the new-file to contain the records as shown below, for example.

transaction-file T update-type	master-file M	new-file N
2476t A	2476	2476t
2477 D	2477	2481
2481 I	2482	2482
2490 D	2483	2483
	2490	2497
	2497	

(The t in 2476t is not part of the employee-number; its purpose is to help us distinguish between the transaction-file record and the master-file record.)

With sequential file updating, the key values of successive records from the master-file and the transaction-file are compared.

```
compare-keys                          example
     if (T = M) then                  T = 2476, M = 2476
          equal-keys
     else if (T <> M) then            T = 2481, M = 2482
          unequal-keys
     endif
```

When the keys are equal, only amendments or deletions should be carried out.

```
equal-keys                            example
     if (update-type = A) then        T = 2476 A, M = 2476
          amend-the-record
     else if (update-type = D) then   T = 2477 D, M = 2477
          delete-the-record
     else
          error(T = M and update-type not A or D)
     endif
```

When the keys are unequal, only insertions or copying the master record to the new-file should be done.

```
unequal-keys                          example
     if (T < M) then                  T = 2481, M = 2482
          insert
     else if (T > M) then
          write-M-to-new              T = 2490, M = 2483
     endif
```

Now, a record should only be inserted if update-type = I.

```
insert                                example
     if (update-type = I) then        T = 2481 I, M = 2482
          insert-the-record
     else
          error (T < M and update-type not I)
     endif
```

Next, amend-the-record, delete-the-record and insert-the-record are detailed. The amendment is effected by writing the amendment record to the new-file.

```
amend-the-record
     write T to new-file
     get-next-T
     get-next M
```

With the deletion, nothing is written to the new-file.

```
delete-the-record
     get-next-T
     get-next-M
```

For the insertion, the record to be inserted is written to the new-file.

```
          insert-the-record
                write T to new-file
                get-next-T
```

And for the case where M is less than T,

```
          write-M-to-new
                write M to new-file
                get-next-M
```

Records can only be retrieved from a file if the end of that file has not been reached.

```
          get-next-T
                if (not at end of transaction file) then
                      retrieve next T
                endif
```

But what if the end of the transaction-file has been reached? We require that the rest of the master-file records (if any) are retrieved and written to the new-file. One way to achieve this is to assign to T the highest-possible-value e.g. 9999. Then the remaining records from the master-file will be written to the new-file because each value of M is less than the value of T. For example, suppose the current values of T and M are 2490 and the value of update-type is D.

	T	M	New	comment
	2490 D	2490		T = M, update-type = D
delete-the-record				
get-next-T	9999			no more records left
get-next-M		2497		in transaction-file,
				so T ← 9999
write-M-to-new				T > M so
write M to new-file			2497	
get-next-M				

If HIGH-VALUE = 9999, then we can write

```
     get-next-T
     if (not end-of-transaction-file) then
           retrieve next T
     else
           T ← HIGH-VALUE
     endif
```

And similarly

```
     get-next-M
          if (not end-of-master-file) then
                retrieve next M
          else
                M <— HIGH-VALUE
          endif
```

Keys are compared until the end of both files is reached.

```
While (T <> HIGH-VALUE or M <> HIGH-VALUE) do
    { terminate loop if both T = 9999 and M = 9999 }
    compare-keys
endwhile
```

Before the loop can be executed for the first time, a record must be retrieved from each file.

```
open master-file for reading in
open transaction-file for reading in
open new-file for writing out
get-next-M
get-next-T
while (T <> HIGH-VALUE or M <> HIGH-VALUE) do
    compare-keys
endwhile
close files
stop
```

get-next-M, get-next-T and compare-keys have already been defined. The complete algorithm is shown next so that it can be understood at a glance.

```
sequential-file-update
    open master-file for reading in
    open transaction-file for reading in
    open new-file for writing out
    get-next-M
    get-next-T
    while (T <> HIGH-VALUE or M <> HIGH-VALUE) do
        compare-keys
    endwhile
    close files
    stop

compare-keys
    if (T = M) then
        equal-keys
    else if (T <> M) then
        unequal-keys
    endif
```

```
equal-keys
    if (update-type = A) then
        amend-the-record
    else if (update-type = D) then
        delete-the-record
    else
        error (T = M and update-type not A or D)
    endif

unequal-keys
    if (T < M) then
        insert
    else if (T > M) then
        write-M-to-new
    endif

insert
    if (update-type = I) then
        insert-the-record
    else
        error (T < M and update-type not I)
    endif

amend-the-record
    write T to new-file
    get-next-T
    get-next M

delete-the-record
    get-next-T
    get-next-M

insert-the-record
    write T to new-file
    get-next-T

write-M-to-new
    write M to new-file
    get-next-M

get-next-T
    if (not end-of-transaction-file) then
        retrieve next T
    else
        T ← HIGH-VALUE
    endif

get-next-M
    if (not end-of-master-file) then
        retrieve next M
    else
        M ← HIGH-VALUE
    endif
```

There is a hierarchy of procedures in this sequential file update algorithm. This hierarchy can be represented by a diagram.

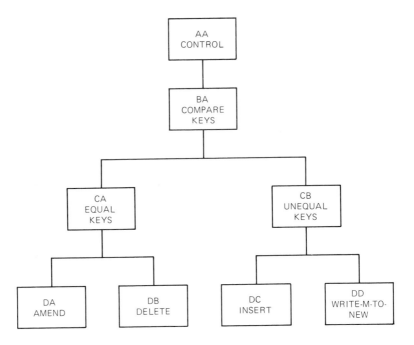

Figure 9.2 Hierachical structure chart for sequential File Update

Figure 9.2 shows the hierarchical arrangement of the main procedures comprising the sequential file update algorithm. It does not show procedures at the lowest level, such as get-next-T, or get-next-M.

This hierarchy of procedures is easily translated into a hierarchy of SECTIONs in a COBOL program, in which a SECTION is PERFORMed by the SECTION above it. Thus, for example, the SECTION BA-COMPARE-KEYS could be written

```
BA-COMPARE-KEYS SECTION.
BA10.
    IF (F2-TRANS-EMP-NUM = F1-MAST-EMP-NUM)
        PERFORM CA-EQUAL-KEYS
    ELSE IF (F2-TRANS-EMP-NUM NOT = F1-MAST-EMP-NUM)
        PERFORM CB-UNEQUAL-KEYS.

CA-EQUAL-KEYS SECTION.
CA10.
    IF (F2-TRANS-UPDATE-TYPE = "A")
        PERFORM DA-AMEND
    etc.
```

Exercise 9.1

1(a) Design, write, test and document a COBOL program which will update a sequential personnel-file from a sequential file of amendment records. The record format in the personnel-file has the structure

> employee-record
> > number   key
> > name
> > department

The record format in the file of amendment records has the same structure apart from an extra field which contains the value A, D or I to indicate the type of amendment record. For the moment, assume that update-types are consistent with the key values. (For example, where key values are equal, the only update-types are either A(mend or D(elete). When devising your test data, pay particular attention to the boundaries of the master and transaction files.

1(b) Where amendment-types are inconsistent with the key values, your program should output the records concerned together with an appropriate message, to the printer, and then retrieve the next pair of records from the master and transaction files. Amend your program so that it meets this requirement. Test and document your amendments.

1(c) The new personnel-file, formed by updating the original personnel-file with the amendment records, becomes the original personnel-file in the next updating session. Arrange for the new personnel-file to take on the external filename of the original personnel-file while, at the same time, preserving the contents of the original personnel-file. (An external filename is the one used by your computer's operating system. It is the name which appears in the disk directory, for example.)

2 A sequential file update will fail if keys (a) are out of order or (b) duplicated. Design, write, test and document a COBOL program which will detect and report on duplicate and out-of-order keys.

9.3 INPUT-OUTPUT ERRORS

If a program attempts to open a file for input and that file does not exist on the disk, or if an attempt is made to create a file on a full disk, then program execution usually terminates and control is returned to the operating system. Robust programs remain in control under such circumstances.

One way to make programs more robust is to make use of the FILE STATUS facility. It forms part of the SELECT clause. For example

```
ENVIRONMENT DIVISION.
INPUT-OUTPUT SECTION.
FILE-CONTROL.
    SELECT F1-MASTER-FILE
        ASSIGN TO DISK
        FILE STATUS IS W-MASTER-FILE-ERROR.
```

W-MASTER-FILE-ERROR is declared in the WORKING-STORAGE SECTION as a two-character alphanumeric data item. (If you are not using the Microsoft COBOL compiler running under the CP/M operating system, consult your manual).

```
WORKING-STORAGE SECTION.
01  W-MASTER-FILE-ERROR  PIC XX.
```

The COBOL run-time system places a value in W-MASTER-FILE-ERROR whenever an OPEN, READ or WRITE statement, refering to F1-MASTER-FILE, is

executed. For example, if the disk space is full and the statement OPEN OUTPUT
F1-MASTER-FILE is executed, W-MASTER-FILE-ERROR would be given a
value, "34" for example, to signify that the disk space is full. This facility allows the
programmer to code something like

```
IF (W-MASTER-FILE-ERROR = "34")
    DISPLAY "Error - disk full. Program execution suspended"
    DISPLAY "PLACE A NEW DISK IN DRIVE"
    DISPLAY "Press return to resume execution"
    DISPLAY "or enter A to abort"
    ACCEPT W-RESPONSE.
```

Exercise 9.2

1 Design, write, test and document small COBOL programs which test file
input–output error trapping procedures. Here are the error codes (called file status
values) provided by the Microsoft COBOL compiler. File status values used by your
compiler might be different — consult your manual.

value	meaning
"00"	successful completion
"10"	end of file encountered
"30"	file not found or disk is corrupt
"34"	disk space full

9.4 SORTING

When a transaction file is created, the records are not necessarily in key field order.
Before a transaction file can be used to update a sequential master file, the records in
the transaction file must be in key field order. If the file is small, then the easiest way
to sort the records would be to hold them in memory (in an array) and then sort the
array. If the file is too large to be held in memory, then an alternative strategy is called
for. One method of sorting large files is the balanced two-way merge sort. The essence
of this sorting method is as follows.

Suppose the key values of records in a file to be sorted are

$$13, 27, 3, 23, 16, 25, 19, 12 \text{ and } 18,$$

and they are held in a file called U (for unsorted). The first step is to split the file in
two, by writing successive records alternately to file A and file B.

U	A	B
13		
27	13	27
3		
23	3	23
16		
25	16	25
19		
12	19	12
18		
	18	

Then, the records are grouped into two, one record from A and one from B, and successive ordered pairs are written alternately to files C and D.

A	B	C	D
13	27	13	
3	23	27	
16	25		3
19	12		23
18		16	
		25	
			12
			19
		18	

Then the records are grouped into four, two records from C and two from D, and the four records are written, in order, to A and B alternately.

C	D	A	B
13		3	
27		13	
	3	23	
	23	27	
16			12
25	12		16
	19		19
			25
18		18	

Then the records are grouped into eight, four records from A and four from B, and the eight records are written, in order, to C and D alternately.

A	B	C	D
3		3	
13		12	
23		13	
27		16	
	12	19	
	16	23	
	19	25	
	25	27	
18			18

And so on until the records are in order.

Only two records are held in memory at any one time. The groups are sorted by merging. The basis of this method is illustrated by showing how files C and D are merged to produce file A.

C	D	A
13		3
27		13
	3	23
	23	27

	From C	From D	A
The first record in each group from C and D is retrieved. Both of these records are the lowest in key order in their group.	13	3	
The record with the lowest key is written out to A and replaced in memory with the next record from the same group.		23	3
This is repeated until the end of one group or the other is reached.	27		13
When the end of one group is reached, the rest of the other group is copied to A.			23
			27

Then the first record in the next group in C and in D is retrieved. This time, the records are written, in order, to B. The whole process is repeated until the end of both C and D is reached.

Exercise 9.3

1 Sort a file of amendment records into key field order by using either the sort utility provided by your compiler or other software, or a program designed and written by yourself which implements the two-way balanced merge.

10
Stacks and Queues

10.1 INTRODUCTION

We have already met some data structures such as arrays and records. There are other data structures and in this chapter we look at some of them.

10.2 STACKS

Many of us have seen a pile of tables, or chairs, stacked one above the other. Stacking tables and chairs are often found in school cafeterias, for example. To get at the fifth table down in a stack, we would first remove the four above it; if the tables were heavy, we would remove them from the stack one by one. The idea of a stack is simple.

A convenient way to represent a stack in a computer is to use an array together with a variable which points to the top of the stack. The top of the stack is where the most recently inserted item is located.

Initially, the stack is empty and top has the value zero.

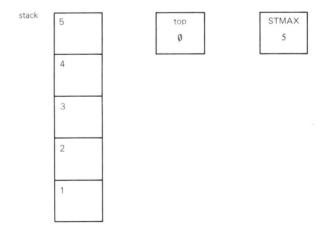

A stack has a finite size. In this example, the maximum size of the stack is constant, and is held in STMAX. Its value is five.

10.2.1 INSERT A NODE

We put the first data item, TOM, on the stack.

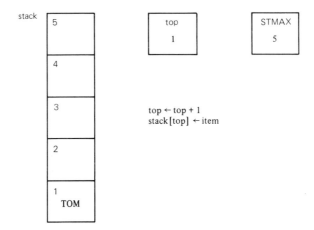

A stack element is called a node. The value of the variable top represents the location of the most recently inserted node. It also represents the current length of the stack, i.e. the number of nodes in the stack. At the moment, this number is one.

We now put two more nodes on the stack.

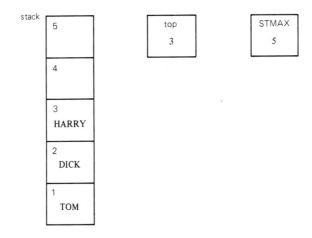

We can put nodes on the stack only if there is room. If the stack is full then both top and STMAX have the same value. So, an attempt to execute

```
top ← top + 1
stack[top] ← item
```

will fail. We guard against this happening by writing

```
if (top = STMAX) then
        error (overflow - stack full)
```

where error is some procedure which signals that the stack is full.

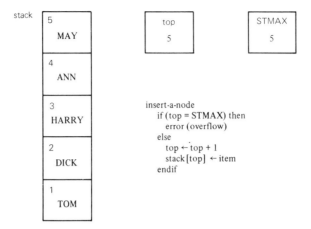

insert-a-node
  if (top = STMAX) then
    error (overflow)
  else
    top ← top + 1
    stack [top] ← item
  endif

10.2.2 DELETE A NODE

If we delete a node from the stack we can imagine

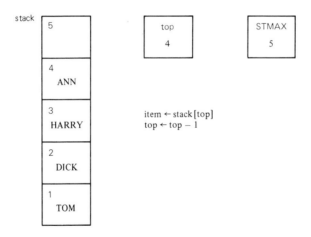

item ← stack [top]
top ← top − 1

Although in fact, the data item MAY physically remains, it is logically removed from the stack by the fact that top now references the fourth position in the array. The fifth position is available for occupation by another item.

Removing the next three nodes from the stack we obtain

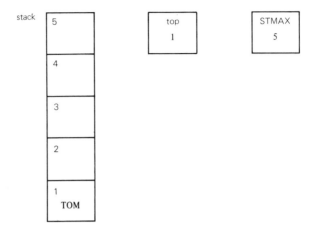

Deleting the last node causes no problems.

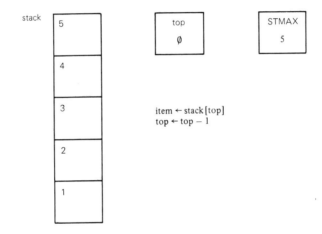

We can delete a node only if the stack is not empty i.e. only if top is not equal to zero. Therefore we write

```
delete-a-node
    if (top = 0) then
            error(underflow - stack empty)
    else
            item ← stack[top]
            top ← top - 1
    endif
```

10.2.3 TRAVERSE A STACK

To visit each node in turn, i.e. traverse the stack, we start with the node at the top of the stack.

```
traverse-stack
    curr ← top
    while (curr <> 0) do
        item ← stack[curr]
        curr ← curr - 1
    endwhile
```

The variable curr references each node in turn i.e. curr refers to the location of the current node being processed. The order of access is last in — first out (abbreviated to LIFO).

10.2.4 PUSHING AND POPPING

Putting nodes on a stack is called pushing. Deleting nodes from a stack is called popping. A stack usually grows and contracts (its number of nodes varies) during its lifetime. This is why a stack is called a dynamic data structure.

Stacks can be used to trace a sequence of events, and then to backtrack along this sequence — as we shall see in the section on binary trees in the next chapter.

Exercise 10.1

1   Implement the following algorithm in COBOL and use it to test COBOL versions of the push and pop procedures.

```
use-stack
    initialise { stack }
    done ← false
    while (done = false) do
        display menu
        if (choice = 1)
            get item from user
            push { item onto stack }
        else if (choice = 2)
            pop { item from stack }
            display item
        else if (choice = 3)
            traverse { traverse and display contents of stack }
        else if (choice = 9)
            done ← true
        endif
    endwhile
    stop
```

Your testing should include pushing and popping the first node, pushing and popping the last node, as well as exercising the underflow and overflow error procedures. These error procedures could take the form

```
display error[n]
```

where error is an array or table comprising two fixed elements.

"overflow - stack full"
and "underflow - stack empty"

If underflow = 2 display error underflow would result in the underflow message being output.

10.3 QUEUES

Think of a queue of people at a food counter in a cafeteria. Newcomers join the rear of the queue. The person at the front of the queue is served first, and is first to leave the queue. A queue is a first in — first out (FIFO) structure.

Initially, the queue is empty. We shall use a one-dimensional array named q to hold the nodes. The variables front and rear indicate the front and rear of the queue. qnum holds the number of nodes in the queue and DMAX holds the maximum size of the queue. Initially, the queue is empty.

10.3.1 INSERT A NODE

We insert the first node at the rear of the queue. Since it is the first node, it is also the front of the queue.

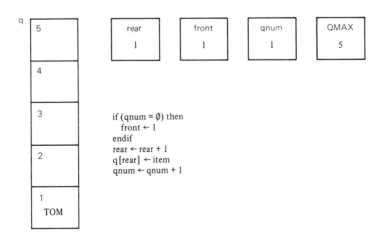

```
if (qnum = Ø) then
    front ← 1
endif
rear ← rear + 1
q[rear] ← item
qnum ← qnum + 1
```

Inserting the next two nodes is straightforward.

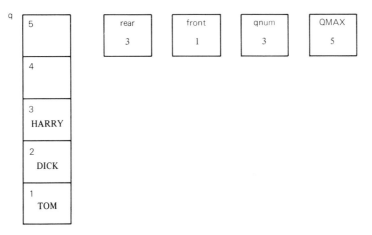

What if the queue is full i.e. what if qnum = QMAX? Then an attempt to insert another node will fail. We have an overflow error condition. Therefore we write

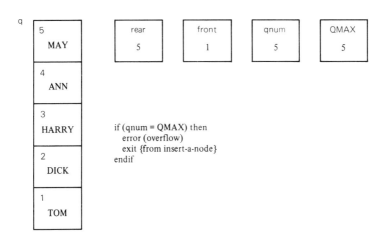

Consider the following situation where three nodes have been removed from the front of a hitherto full queue. (We shall see how to delete nodes from a queue in the next section.) The front of the queue is now in the fourth position in the array. How can we insert the next node?

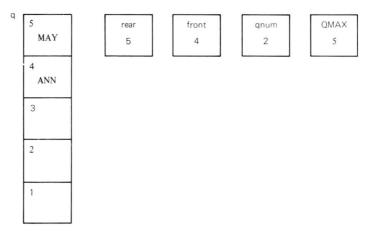

We could arrange for the queue to wrap around the array, so that the next node is placed in position one of the array.

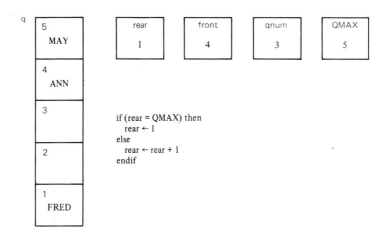

We can now assemble the algorithm for inserting nodes into a queue.

```
insert-a-node
      if (qnum = QMAX) then                    { queue is full }
            error(overflow)
            exit { insert-a-node }
      endif
      if (qnum = Ø) then                        { first node }
            front ← 1
      endif
      if (rear = QMAX) then                     { wrap round }
            rear ← 1
      else
            rear ← rear + 1
      endif
      q[rear] ← item                            { insert at rear of queue }
      qnum ← qnum + 1
```

10.3.2 DELETE A NODE

Suppose we now want to delete the node from the front of this queue.

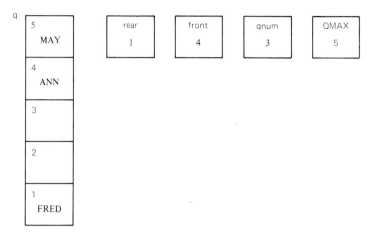

This is quite straightforward.

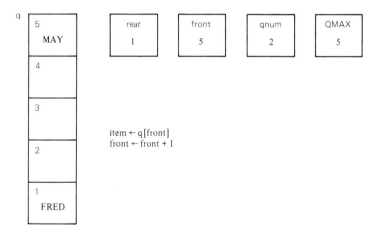

item ← q[front]
front ← front + 1

If the node to be removed is in the fifth position in the array, then we need to take wrap around into account i.e. we need to set front to one.

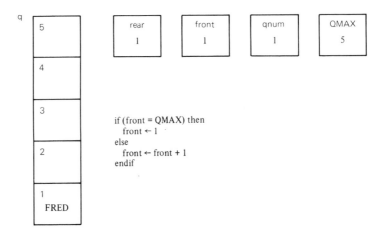

Finally, we can delete nodes from a queue only if there are nodes to delete.

```
delete-a-node
      If (qnum = 0) then                        { nothing to delete }
            error(underflow)
            exit { delete-a-node }
      endif
      item ← q[front]                           { delete from front }
      if (front = QMAX) then                     { wrap round }
            front ← 1
      else
            front ← front + 1
      endif
      qnum ← qnum - 1
```

10.3.3 APPLICATIONS

Uses of queues include maintaining a set of computer jobs waiting to use the printer (i.e. spooling) and modelling situations where queues occur, for example in a cafeteria or at road traffic lights. Often, these models can be used to help improve efficiency. For example, they could be used to help answer questions such as: if an extra cash till was installed, then what would be the average time a customer would have to wait in the queue; if queues were shorter, would more people use the cafeteria and would the extra custom pay for another till and cashier?

Exercise 10.2

1   Design and test an algorithm which will traverse a queue. You should ensure that your algorithm behaves sensibly when the queue
   (a) is empty
   (b) contains one node
   (c) is full

2   Design, write and test an interactive COBOL program which will maintain a queue data structure (i.e. insert and delete nodes). Your program should also traverse the queue and display its contents in the order in which the items were inserted.

11

Linked Lists and Binary Trees

11.1 INTRODUCTION

In Chapter 10, we looked at stacks and queues as examples of dynamic data structures. In this chapter, we look at two more dynamic data structures, linked lists and binary trees.

11.2 LINKED LISTS

A linked list is used to maintain a list of data items in, for example, alphabetical order. In a linked list, each node has two parts — data fields, and a link (or pointer) field. The pointer field holds the address of the next node in order. For example,

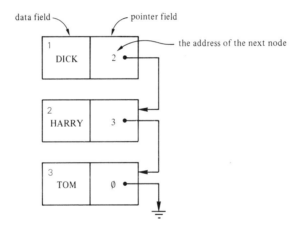

Node one points to (i.e. contains the address of) node two. Node two points to node three. Node three points to nothing — it has a null link to indicate that there are no more nodes in the list.

We use two arrays — namelist for the data, and linklist for the pointer. Thus, for example, node three comprises namelist[3] and linklist[3]. free points to the first node in the list of free nodes. start points to the first name in alphabetical order. LMAX holds the value of the maximum number of nodes that can be held. curr refers to the current node being processed. Initially, the namelist is empty and all the nodes are free, i.e. available for use.

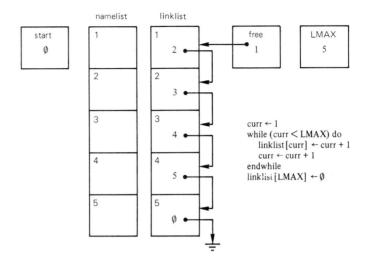

11.2.1 INSERT A NODE

It might be worth your while reading this section twice — the first time following the text and the diagrams to obtain an understanding of the principles involved, and the second time dry running the algorithms to appreciate the details.

We insert the first node by storing the data item in the next free node and then adjusting the pointers. curr preserves the value of free during this process, and refers to the current node being processed.

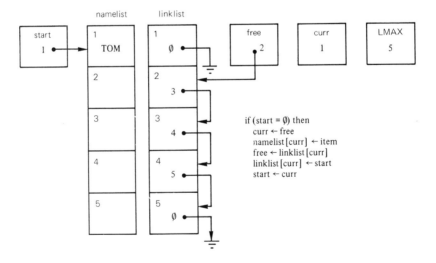

The algorithm shows how we arrive at the current state from the previous state. The three statements

```
free ← linklist[curr]
linklist[curr] ← start
start ← curr
```

identify the next free node.

We insert the next node. The data item is DICK. DICK comes before TOM in alphabetical order.

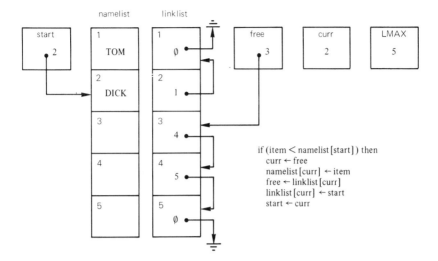

Next, we want to insert HARRY, which comes between TOM and DICK. First, we assign HARRY to the next free node.

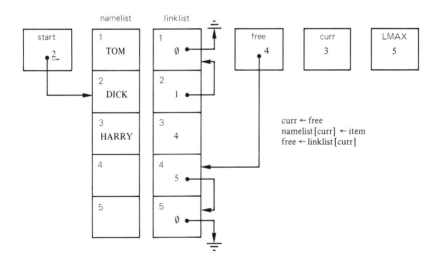

Then, we traverse the list, looking for the logical position for HARRY. We do this by starting with the node pointed at by start, then following the links (which trace the names in alphabetical order) until we reach TOM, the name which logically follows HARRY.

```
k ← start
while (item >= namelist[k]) do
      j ← k
      k ← linklist[k]
endwhile
```

It is worth your while pausing to dry run this algorithm so that you can clearly see what is happening.

start	k	item	namelist[k]	J
2	2	HARRY	DICK	2
	1		TOM	

The value of start (2) is assigned to k. The item (HARRY) is greater than namelist[k] (DICK) so we enter the loop. The value of k (2) is assigned to j, and the value of linklist[k] (1) is assigned to k. We come to the top of the loop again. The item (HARRY) is not greater than namelist[k] (DICK), so the loop terminates.

If $k = 0$, then linklist[k] is undefined. So we write

> while (k <> 0) and (item >= namelist[k]) do
> etc.

Finally, we adjust the pointers.

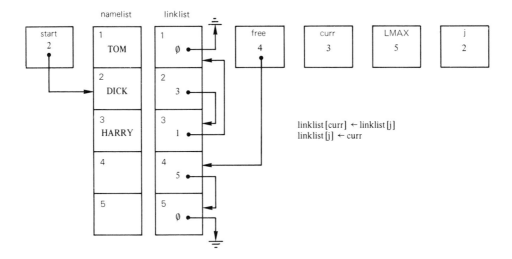

linklist [curr] ← linklist [j]
linklist [j] ← curr

Remembering that we cannot insert a node if there are no free nodes i.e. if free points to nothing, we can now assemble the algorithm for inserting a node into a linked list.

```
insert-a-node
      if (free = 0) then                                     { list is full }
            error(overflow)
      else if (start = 0) then                               { insert first node }
            curr ← free
            namelist[curr] ← item
            free ← linklist[curr]
            linklist[curr] ← start
            start ←  curr
      else if (item < namelist[start])                       { insert before first node }
            curr ← free
            namelist[curr] ← item
            free ← linklist[curr]
            linklist[curr] ← start
            start ← curr
   else                                                      { insert after first node }
            curr ← free
            namelist[curr] item
            free ← linklist[curr]
            k ← start                                        { traverse list }
            while (k <> 0 ) and (item >= namelist[k]) do
                  j ← k
                  k ← linklist[k]
            endwhile
            linklist[curr] ← linklist[j]                     { adjust pointers }
            linklist[j] ← curr
      endif
```

Exercise 11.1

1 By using diagrams, show how a node can be inserted, i.e. how a name of your choice can be included in the linked list.

11.2.2 DELETE A NODE

Suppose we want to delete DICK from this linked list.

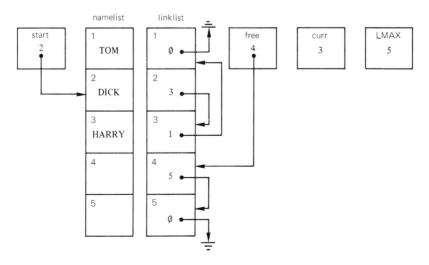

We return the node occupied by DICK to the list of free nodes.

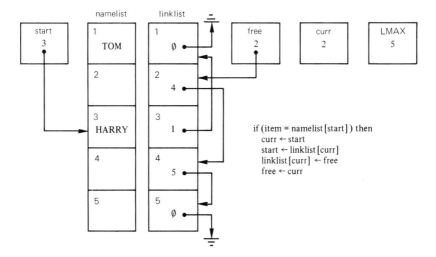

Now, we shall delete TOM, physically the first item in the list. First, we locate the position of the item (TOM) in the linked list.

```
k ← start
while (k <> 0) and (item <> namelist[k]) do
    j ← k
    k ← linklist[k]
endwhile
```

Tracing the changing values of k and j as the position of TOM is located,

```
k      j
3      3
1
```

Then, if the item (TOM) cannot be found, we output an appropriate message, otherwise we adjust the pointers and return the node to the free list.

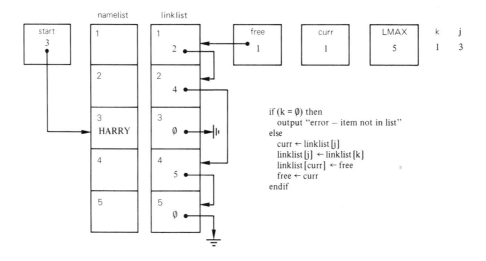

We now assemble the algorithm for deleting a node from a linked list.

```
delete-a-node
    if (start = 0) then                     { empty linked list }
        error(underflow)
    else if (item = namelist[start]) then   { delete first node }
        curr ← start
        start ← linklist[curr]
        linklist[curr] ← free
        free ← curr
    else                                    { delete other nodes }
        k ← start                           { traverse list }
        while (k <> 0) and (item <> namelist[k]) do
            j ← k
            k ← linklist[k]
        endwhile
        if (k = 0) then
            output "error — item not in list"
        else                                { adjust pointers }
            curr ← linklist[j]
            linklist[j] ← linklist[k]
            linklist[curr] ← free
            free ← curr
        endif
    endif
```

Exercise 11.2

1 By using diagrams, show how a node can be deleted from a linked list.

2 Design, write, test and document a COBOL program which maintains a register of competitors in a marathon. (The maximum number of competitors is restricted to fifty.) Since competitors may register or withdraw at any time up to the day before the event, and since the list must be maintained in alphabetical order at all times, a linked list would be an appropriate data structure. Your program should be able to list the competitors, in alphabetical order, who have not withdrawn. You should use arrays, together with the necessary data items, to represent the linked list.

11.3 BINARY TREES

A linked list is useful for maintaining a list of data items in, say, alphabetical order. But searching for a particular item in a linked list involves looking at each list item in turn until the required one is found or the end of the list is reached. This can take an unacceptably long time. With a binary tree, the time taken to locate an item is usually less, and the data items can still be maintained in, say, alphabetical order.

A node in a binary tree comprises data fields and pointer or link fields.

left link	data item	right link

The pointer variables left and right are used to point to other nodes, i.e. to contain the addresses of other nodes. This is shown in the following pointer representation of a binary tree.

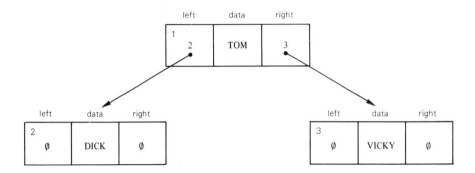

Node one's left pointer points to node two. Node one's right pointer points to node three. Node three's left and right pointers both have a null value: they point to nothing. We shall use arrays to represent pointer and data fields. BTMAX is the maximum number of nodes in the binary tree.

Initially, free has the value one and refers to the first free node, and curr has the value zero and refers to the current node being processed.

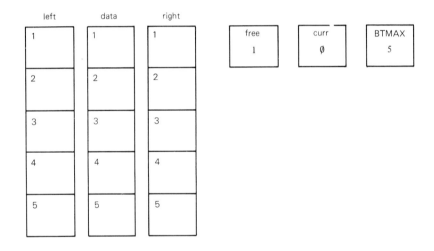

11.3.1 INSERT A NODE

We begin by inserting TOM.

The following diagram shows this insertion in terms of arrays.

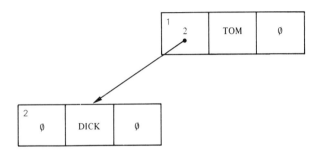

```
if (curr = ∅) then
    curr ← free
    data[curr] ← item
    left[curr] ← ∅
    right[curr] ← ∅
    free ← free + 1
```

Next, we insert DICK.

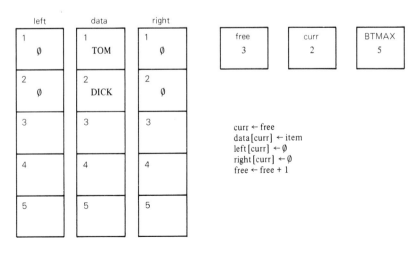

DICK comes before TOM in alphabetical order. So DICK is placed in the next free node to the left of TOM's. We show how this may be accomplished using arrays. First, we insert the node.

```
curr ← free
data[curr] ← item
left[curr] ← ∅
right[curr] ← ∅
free ← free + 1
```

Then we traverse the tree looking for the logical position for this node.

```
k ← 1                                           { traverse tree }
while (k <> 0) do
      j ← k
      if (item < data[k]) then                  { go left }
            k ← left[k]
            insert ← left
      else
            .
            .
            .
      endif
endwhile
```

We step through this traversal algorithm to trace the changing values of k and j.

$$
\begin{array}{cc}
k & j \\
1 & 1 \\
0 &
\end{array}
$$

Finally, we adjust the pointers.

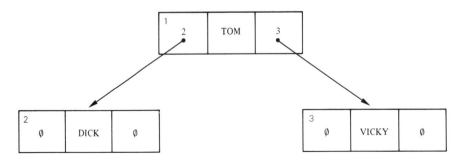

left		data		right	
1	2	1	TOM	1	0
2	0	2	DICK	2	0
3		3		3	
4		4		4	
5		5		5	

free	curr	BTMAX	j
3	2	5	1

```
if (insert = left) then { adjust left pointer}
      left[j] ← curr
else .
      .
      .
```

That completes the insertion of DICK. Next, we insert the data item VICKY. VICKY comes after TOM in alphabetical order. So VICKY is assigned to the next free node to the right of TOM's.

Using arrays:

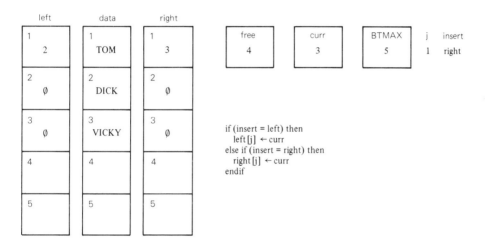

```
curr ← free              {item into next free node}
data[curr] ← item
left[curr] ← ∅
right[curr] ← ∅
free ← free + 1
k ← 1                    {traverse tree}
while (k <> ∅) do
    j ← k
    if (item < data[k]) then {go left}
        k ← left[k]
        insert ← left
    else                 {go right}
        k ← right[k]
        insert ← right
    endif
endwhile
```

Adjusting pointers:

```
if (insert = left) then
    left[j] ← curr
else if (insert = right) then
    right[j] ← curr
endif
```

The next data item to insert is HARRY. HARRY comes before TOM, so we go to the left of TOM. But HARRY comes after DICK, so we go to the right of DICK.

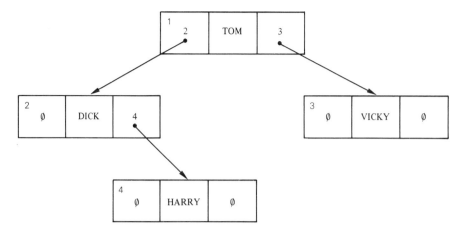

The array representation for inserting Harry is

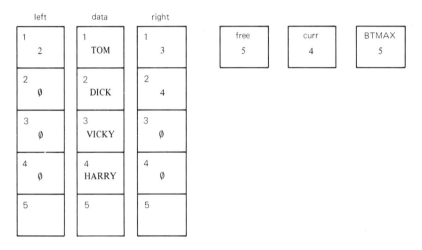

Finally, we insert ANN. ANN comes before TOM, so we go to the left of TOM. ANN comes before DICK. So we place ANN to the left of DICK.

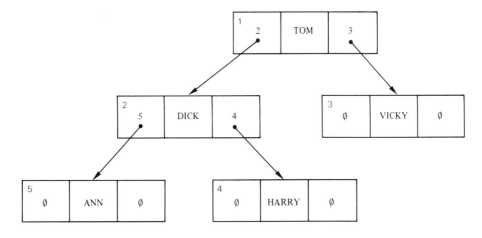

Alternatively:

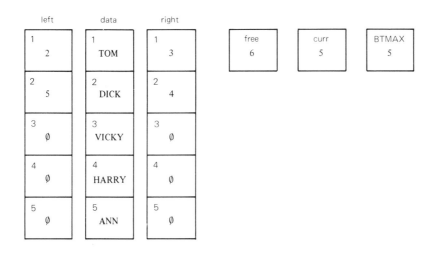

We can now specify an algorithm for inserting a node in a binary tree.

```
insert-a-node
    if (free > BTMAX) then
        error(overflow)
    else if (curr = 0) then              { insert root node }
        curr ← free
        data[curr] ← item
        left[curr] ← 0
        right[curr] ← 0
        free ← free + 1
    else                                 { insert node }
        curr ← free
        data[curr] ← item
        left[curr] ← 0
        right[curr] ← 0
        free ← free + 1
        k ← 1                            { traverse tree }
        while (k <> 0) do
            j ← k
            if (item < data[k]) then     { go left }
                k ← left[k]
                insert ← left
            else                         { go right }
                k ← right[k]
                insert ← right
            endif
        endwhile
        if (insert = left) then          { adjust left pointer }
            left[j] ← curr
        else if (insert = right) then    { adjust right pointer }
            right[j] ← curr
        endif
    endif
```

11.3.2 IN-ORDER TRAVERSAL

In this section, we see how to traverse a binary tree in alphabetical order of its data items. The essential idea is this. We start at the top node. Then we go left as far as we can and display the data item (ANN). Then we backtrack to the preceding node, display its data item (DICK) and go right. We use a stack to record the nodes that have been visited.

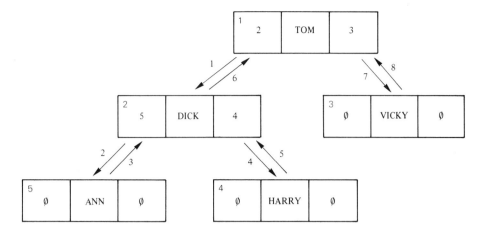

The arrows show the order in which the nodes are visited in in-order traversal.
start holds the address of the root node, namely one. curr refers to the node currently being visited. top is a pointer to the top of the stack. Initially,

```
start ← 1
curr ← start
top ← 0
```

Then we go left as far as we can, storing the address of each node visited on a stack.

```
while (curr <> 0) do { go left and stack the current node }
        top ← + 1
        stack [top] ← curr
        curr ← left[curr]
endwhile
```

The dry run is

start	curr	top	curr<>0?	stack[top]	left[curr]
1	1	0	true		
		1		1	2
	2		true		
		2		2	5
	5		true		
		3		5	0
	0		false		

Initially, start = 1, curr = 1, top = 0 and (curr<>0) is true. So we go into the loop.
   top is incremented by 1 — its value is now 1, the value of curr (1) is assigned to stack[1] and the value of left[1] (2) is assigned to curr. The condition (curr<>0) is met, so we go into the loop.

top is incremented by 1 — its value is now 3. the value of left[5] (0) is assigned to curr. The condition (curr<>0) is not met (because curr = 0) so we terminate the loop.

The address of each node encountered in going left as far as possible, namely 1, 2 and 4, has been placed on the stack.

Then, we display the data item whose address is at the top of the stack, pop the stack (we have finished with this address) and find the address of the next node on the right.

top has the value 3 and the condition (top<>0) is met. So the value of stack[3] (5) is assigned to curr, data[5] (ANN) is displayed, 1 is substracted from top and the value of right[5] (0) is assigned to curr.

The dry run is

top	top<>0?	stack [top]	curr	data[curr]	right- [curr]
3	true				
2		5	5	ANN	0
			0		

```
if (top <> 0) then
    curr ← stack[top]
    display data [curr]
    curr ← right[curr]
    top ← top - 1
endif
```

We now present an algorithm for traversing the nodes of an ordered binary tree in alphabetical (or numerical) order.

```
traverse-in-order
    start ← 1                                    { initialise }
    curr ← start
    top ← 0
    while (top <> 0) and (curr <> 0) do
        { if top = 0 and curr = 0, then all nodes have been visited }
        while (curr <> 0) do { go left and stack the current node }
            top ← top + 1
            stack[top] ← curr
            curr ← left[curr]
        endwhile
        if (top <> 0) then                       { display, go right, pop }
            curr ← stack[top]
            display data [curr]
            curr ← right[curr]
            top ← top - 1
        endif
    endwhile
```

11.3.3 DELETE A NODE

Perhaps the simplest way to delete a node is to mark the node as having been deleted — but to leave it physically in the tree with its pointers intact. This can be achieved by giving each node an extra field called deleted, say. Then deleted can be given the value false when the node is created, and the value true when the node is (logically) deleted. The delete-a-node algorithm then is essentially

> traverse tree until required node is found
> set delete to true.

11.3.4 NOTATION

We introduce some commonly used terms. Refer to the diagram on page 125 of our binary tree. Node one is called the *root* node. In our example, node one has two *children*: the left child in node two, and the right child in node three. Node two has one child: namely node four. The *parent* of node four is node two. Nodes two and three have a common parent in node one. The *root* node has no parent. The lines joining the nodes are called *branches*. An *ordered* binary tree is one in which any left child precedes, either alphabetically or numerically, its parent and, if it exists, the right child. The binary trees referred to in this chapter are all ordered binary trees.

Exercise 11.2

1 Dry run the traverse–in–order algorithm using the example binary tree given on page 127.

2 Design, write and test a COBOL program which will maintain an ordered binary tree of names, and will list the names (except the deleted ones) in ascending order.

3 Design, write, test and document a program to help a doctor identify a particular person's record, according to the following specification.

A record in an indexed file of patient's details has the structure

patient-record

record-number	key — uniquely identifies record
surname	several patients may have the same surname
nhs-number	national health service number
rest-of-record	first-two-forenames, address, sex, date-of birth

Surname-index is another file. A record in this file has the structure

index-record

node-number	key — uniquely identifies the record
left	pointer to left child
right	pointer to right child
deleted	value true or false
name	same as surname in patients-details file
pointer-to-recnum	pointer to record-number in patients-details file

The contents of the surname-index file is read into a binary tree data structure held in memory. When the doctor enters a surname, the binary tree is searched for names which match this surname. For each matching name found, the corresponding value of pointer-to-recnum is used as the key field value to retrieve a patient-record from the patients-details file. The forenames, nhs-number, address, sex and date-of-birth of each patient with the same surname as the one entered by the doctor is displayed.

When a new patient is added to the doctor's list, or removed from it, both the surname-index file and the patients-details file are updated.

12

Structured Programming and Stepwise Refinement

12.1 INTRODUCTION

When we design an algorithm, we aim to produce one which
 does the required job
 is free from unexpected errors
 is easy to understand
 is easy to modify

Structured programming and stepwise refinement help achieve these aims.

12.2 STRUCTURED PROGRAMMING

Structured programming is designing and writing programs using sequences, selections, repetitions and module calls.

12.2.1 SEQUENCES

A sequence is a list of statements, each of which specifies some action to be carried out or executed. The statements are executed in the order given. For example,

```
set count to 0
open file for reading
output headings
```

is a sequence of statements.

12.2.2 SELECTIONS

A selection allows a particular sequence of statements to be selected for execution.

```
if (quantity-in-stock <= re-order-level) then
    copy stock-item-code to re-order-code
    copy todays-date to re-order-date
endif
```

The two copy statements are selected for execution only if the condition (quantity-in-stock <= re-order-level) is met. This is easily written to COBOL.

```
IF (QUANTITY-IN-STOCK < RE-ORDER-LEVEL OR = RE-ORDER-LEVEL)
    MOVE STOCK-ITEM-CODE TO RE-ORDER-CODE
    MOVE TODAYS-DATE TO RE-ORDER-DATE.
```

Notice that the endif becomes a full stop in COBOL.

In the next example, either one statement-sequence or the other is selected for execution.

```
if (name-found = false) then
        write 'name not found'
else
        write 'name found'
        output name-record
endif
```

If the condition (name-found = false) is met, then 'name not found' is displayed. If the condition (name-found = false) is not met, then 'name found' is displayed and the record is output (to the printer, say). In structured English, it is reasonable to use the programming or American term else instead of the English word otherwise provided the meaning remains clear to the reader. Writing this in COBOL we obtain

```
IF  (NAME-FOUND = "FALSE")
        DISPLAY NAME " not found"
ELSE
        DISPLAY NAME " found"
        WRITE PRINTLINE FROM NAME-RECORD.
```

Mistakes are less likely to be made if the statement-sequence following the else is longer than the statement-sequence following the if. This is because a tiny else clause at the end of a long sequence of statements is easily missed by a human reader.

A statement-sequence can itself be a selection. The next example could be part of an algorithm which determines the level of access to patients' records in a hospital. (For example, a ward clerk would be allowed access to a patient's non-medical details such as name, address and date of birth; medical staff would be allowed access to these details and to the patient's medical history.)

```
if (password-1 = ok) then
        if (password-2 = ok) then { password-1 ok and password-2 ok }
            print 'full access permission granted'
        else { password-1 ok but password-2 not ok }
            print 'limited access permission granted'
else { password-1 not ok }
        print 'no access permission granted'
endif
```

Non-medical staff enter one password. Medical staff enter two passwords. Full access is granted if both passwords are ok. If password-1 is ok, but password-2 is not ok, then only partial access is granted. If password-1 is not ok, then no access whatsoever is granted. The comments contained inside the curly brackets are included to help make the meaning clear. In COBOL,

```
IF  (PASSWORD-1 = "OK")
        IF (PASSWORD-2 = "OK")
            DISPLAY "Full access permission granted"
        ELSE
            DISPLAY "Limited access permission granted"
ELSE
        DISPLAY "No access permission granted".
```

Notice that each else is paired with its nearest preceeding unmatched if. The indentation makes this clear to the reader.

In the next example, only one of several alternatives is selected.

```
case amend-type of
        a : amend-a-record
        i : insert-a-record
        d : delete-a-record
        else
                amend-type-error
endcase
```

If amend-type has the value a, then amend-a-record is executed. If amend-type has the value i, then insert-a-record is executed. If amend-type has the value d, then delete-a-record is executed. If the value of amend-type is not one from the set of valid amend-type values (a, i and d) then amend-type-error is executed. Only one of these cases is executed. Once a case has been executed, control passes to the statement following the endcase. The case construction can be written in COBOL as a chain of ELSE IF's.

```
IF (AMEND-TYPE = "A")
    PERFORM AMEND-A-RECORD
ELSE IF (AMEND-TYPE = "I")
    PERFORM INSERT-A-RECORD
ELSE IF (CHOICE = "D")
    PERFORM DELETE-A-RECORD
ELSE
    PERFORM AMEND-TYPE-ERROR.
```

Understanding a chain of ELSE IF's is easy. Look down the list until you come across the first condition that is satisfied, execute the corresponding instruction, then do the sentence following the full stop.

12.2.3 REPETITIONS

Repetitions (or loops) allow for a statement-sequence to be executed a number of times. Sometimes, the precise number of times is known. For example, suppose an array held the names of the exams to be set on each day during a week and it was appropriate to display them.

```
day ← 0
repeat 5 times
        add 1 to day
        output exam-schedule[day]
endrepeat
```

The variable day is used to address or index the array, i.e. day is used as a subscript. Initially, it is set to zero. Then day is incremented by one and the exam-schedule for that day is output. The two processes, increment day and output exam-schedule, are repeated five times altogether. One way of writing this in COBOL is

```
LOOP-CONTROL.
        MOVE 0 TO W-DAY
        PERFORM LOOP 5 TIMES
        GO TO NEXT-PARA.
    LOOP.
        ADD 1 TO W-DAY
        DISPLAY EXAM-SCHEDULE (W-DAY).
    NEXT-PARA.
```

COBOL maintains a count of the number of times LOOP has been executed. When LOOP has been executed the required number of times, control passes to the next sentence, namely GO TO NEXT-PARA.

The following algorithm repeats a statement-sequence until a condition is met.

```
repeat
      get reply
      if (reply in [a..z, A..Z]) then
            reply-ok ← true
      else
            reply-ok ← false
      endif
until (reply-ok = true)
```

The statements get reply and if reply in . . . are executed. reply-ok is assigned either the value true or the value false. Then reply-ok is tested. If the condition (reply-ok = true) is not met, then the statements get reply and if (reply in . .) are executed again, and the condition re-tested. If the condition (reply-ok = true) is met, then control passes to the statement following the until clause. The statements bracketed between repeat and until are executed at least once. One way of writing this in COBOL is

```
INPUT-CONTROL.
      PERFORM GET-REPLY
      PERFORM GET-REPLY UNTIL (REPLY-OK  = "TRUE")
      GO TO NEXT-PARA.
GET-REPLY.
      ACCEPT ANSWER.
      IF (ANSWER ALPHABETIC)
            MOVE "TRUE" TO REPLY-OK
      ELSE
            MOVE "FALSE" TO REPLY-OK.
NEXT-PARA.
```

GET-REPLY is executed for the first time and REPLY-OK is assigned a value. Then this value is used to determine whether GET-REPLY should be executed again. With PERFORM paragraph UNTIL (condition), the condition is tested first to determine whether the paragraph should be executed; and it is tested again each time before the paragraph can be executed. GET-REPLY is executed at least once.

Testing a condition before each repetition is usually the most robust form of loop control i.e. is usually the least likely to cause unforeseen problems.

```
input name
while (name not terminating-value) do
      input address
      write record to file
      input name
endwhile
```

A value is given to name. If it is the terminating-value, then control is passed to the statement following endwhile; if it is not the terminating-value, then the address is input and the record written to the file. Then another value for name is input and the condition (name not terminating-value) re-tested. Whether the statements bracketed between while and endwhile are executed depends on the value of the condition. Because the condition is evaluated before the statements can be executed, it is possible for these statements not to be executed at all. One way of writing this in COBOL is

```
LOOP-CONTROL.
     ACCEPT NAME
     PERFORM LOOP UNTIL (NAME = TERMINATING-VALUE)
     GO TO NEXT-PARA.
LOOP.
     ACCEPT ADDRESS
     WRITE NAME-ADDRESS-RECORD
     ACCEPT NAME.
NEXT-PARA.
```

Notice that in the structured English while (condition) do, the condition is for the loop to be executed. In the COBOL PERFORM paragraph UNTIL (condition), the condition is for the loop to be terminated. It is possible that, depending on the value of NAME, LOOP is not executed at all.

A statement-sequence can itself be a repetition. For example, suppose the following table were to be output from a two-dimensional array onto the screen.

	Mon	Tue	Wed	Thu	Fri
9-11	COBOL	Pascal	hardware	o/systems	packages
11-1	COBOL	Pascal	data proc	data stru	algorithms

Essentially, the algorithm is: for each row, print the column entry.

```
for each row { there are three rows }
     for each column { there are six columns }
          print table item
     endfor
     newline
endfor
```

In more detail,

```
row ← 1
while (row <= 3) do
     col ← 1
     while (col <= 6) do
          output table[row, col]
          add 1 to col
     endwhile
     newline
     add 1 to row
endwhile
```

The table is printed row by row, and, for each row, column by column. One way of programming this loop within a loop in COBOL is

```
DISPLAY-TABLE.
    MOVE 1 TO W-ROW
    PERFORM PRINT-LINE UNTIL (W-ROW > 3)
    GO TO NEXT-PARA.

PRINT-LINE.
    MOVE 1 TO W-COL
    PERFORM PRINT-COL UNTIL (W-COL > 6)
    ADD 1 TO W-ROW.

PRINT-COL.
    DISPLAY TABLE-ENTRY (W-ROW, W-COL)
    ADD 1 TO W-COL.

NEXT-PARA.
```

Of course, screen formatting statements would be required in order to display each table entry in its correct position. These have been omitted in order not to confuse the issue.

12.2.4 MODULE CALLS

In order not to clutter up algorithms with too much detail, we might write something like

```
case amend-type of
    a : amend-a-record
    i : insert-a-record
    d : delete-a-record
    else
            amend-type-error
endcase
```

where, for example, amend-a-record represents an algorithm stated in more detail elsewhere. An algorithm is referred to by underlining its name. In COBOL, algorithms may be referred to by their paragraph name or sequence of paragraph names, by their SECTION name, or by their program name. Paragraphs or SECTIONS are PERFORMed, and programs are CALLed or CHAINed. This is the subject of Chapter 15 — Modular Programming.

12.3 THE GO-TO STATEMENT

The go-to statement is avoided in structured programming because its excessive or ill-considered use makes programs hard for humans to understand. Here are some guidelines on its use.

Use a go-to to branch to a point further on in a program only if it makes the program simpler and easier to follow.

Never use a go-to to branch to an earlier point in a program — for this forms a loop. Loop constructions, such as while (condition) do, are much clearer.

In COBOL, the target of a GO TO statement should be a paragraph name, never a SECTION name.

12.4 STEPWISE REFINEMENT

Stepwise refinement is a method of designing algorithms. Essentially, the method is: start with a simple outline written in English, repeatedly refine it by adding more detail until the algorithm reaches the stage where it can easily be coded in a programming language.

Example

A college maintains a serial file of people who have expressed an interest in joining an evening course in computing. Records predating 1985 are to be removed from the file on the assumption that these people are no longer interested in joining a course. The purged records are to be listed for reference, and the remaining records are to be written to two serial files, one for people interested in programming, the other for people whose interest is business packages. Design and write the program which will purge the file and produce the listing.

The record format includes the following fields.

  (i)   date of enquiry
 (ii)   name
(iii)   address
 (iv)   phone number
  (v)   interest {programming or packages}

We start by establishing WHAT needs to be done. Re-stating the question in terms of the outputs required and the inputs available we obtain

To produce   (a) a listing (report) of all records removed (purged) from the file
        and (b) a serial file of people remaining on file who are interested in programming
        and (c) a serial file of people remaining on file who are interested in business packages.

From   (a) a serial file of people interested in computing.

We can represent these requirements in a diagram.

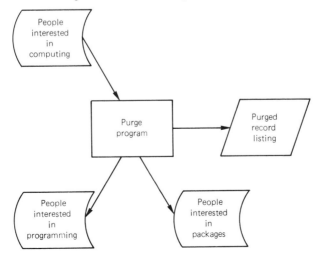

Next we turn our attention to the outputs because these determine the goals of our programming efforts. We start with the report format — see Figure 12.1. Then we specify the content and structure of the files. These are derived from the enquiries file used for input.

```
enquiry-file                          serial organisation
    enquiry-record
        date-of-enquiry
            day                       2 numeric
            month                     3 alphabetic
            year                      2 numeric
        name                          20 alphanum
        address                       50 alphanum
        phone-number                  20 alphanum
        interest                      2-character code: pr programming
                                                        pa packages


programming-enquiry-file              serial organisation
    prog-enquiry-record
        date-of-enquiry
        name
        address
        phone-number

packages-enquiry-file — as for programming-enquiry-file
```

Now we turn out attention to HOW the job is to be done. We start by relating the input to the output.

```
retrieve first enquiry–record
while (not end of enquiry-file) do
    if (year < 85) then
        write-record-to-printer
    else if (interest = pr) { programming }
        write enquiry-record to prog-enquiry-file
    else if (interest = pa) { packages }
        write enquiry-record to pack-enquiry-file
    endif
    retrieve next enquiry-record
endwhile
```

This prompts us to make a note that our test data should include records with years 84, 85 and 86 — to test the boundary around 1985 — and that our test data should include year 87 together with interests pr, pa and neither pr nor pa. This suggests that we should include the default case, else error (year >= 85 and invalid interest).

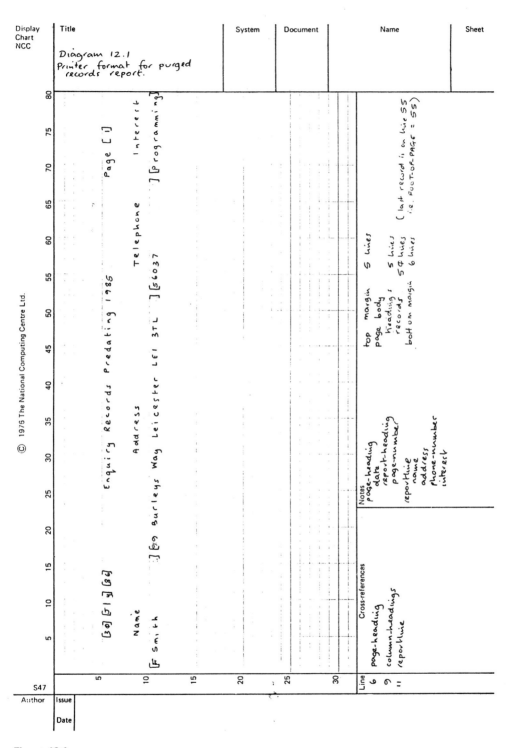

Figure 12.1

```
retrieve first enquiry–record
while (not end of enquiry-file) do
        if (year < 85) then
                write-record-to-printer
        else if (interest = pr) then
                write enquiry-record to prog-enquiry-file
        else if (interest = pa)
                write enquiry-record to pack-enquiry-file
                else
                        error(year >= 85 and invalid interest)
                endif
        retrieve next enquiry-record
        endwhile
```

Now we attend to the details of write–record–to–printer. The first record should be wirtten on a new page. If we are at the end of a page, the record should be written on the next page.

```
write-record-to-printer
        if (end-of-page = true) then
                newpage
        endif
        output reportline {i.e. the record to be printed}
        add 1 to line-number
        if (line-number > FOOT-OF-PAGE) then
                end-of-page ← true
        endif
```

Next, we consider details of newpage. We do not know how to get to the next page — yet. So we write

```
newpage
        nextpage
        output headings
        add 1 to page-number
        line-number ← 1
        end-of-page ← false
```

And now, nextpage. This is easy!

```
nextpage
        output bottom margin of current page { LINES-AT-BOT blank lines }
        output top margin of next page { LINES-AT-TOP blank lines }
```

The algorithm developed so far suggests the constants we need to define, the variables we need to initialise, the files we need to open and some more test data.

(a) 49 records
(b) 50 records   all with year < 85 – to test that paging
(c) 51 records   works ok (50 records per page)

```
startup
    FOOT-OF-PAGE ← 50
    LINES-AT-TOP ← 5
    LINES-AT-BOT ← 6
    page-number ← 1
    end-of-page ← true
    open enquiry-file for reading in
    open prog-enquiry-file for writing out
    open pack-enquiry-file for writing out
    open printer-file for writing out
    retrieve first record from enquiry-file
    if (end of enquiry-file) then
        error (no records in the input file - run abandoned)
        close all files
        stop
    endif
```

In startup we retrieved the first enquiry-record from the enquiry-file. So we write

```
purge-enquiry-file
    startup
    while (not end of enquiry-file) do
        if (year < 85) then
            write-record-to-printer
        else if (interest = pr) then
            write enquiry-record to prog-enquiry-file
        else if (interest = pa) then
            write enquiry-record to pack-enquiry-file
        else
            error (year >= 85 and invalid interest)
        endif
        retrieve next enquiry-record
    endwhile
    closedown
```

closedown is easy.

```
closedown
    close all files
    stop
```

At this point, we have probably included enough detail to enable us to write the COBOL program quite comfortably since only a little more thought is required to complete the task. For example, output reportline would involve MOVEing appropriate fields to the reportline before writing it to the printer, nextpage, would involve outputting the page-heading AFTER ADVANCING PAGE.

This solution is not necessarily the best one, nor the most rigorous. But it is adequate for our purposes — to demonstrate a program design method.

Any method of repeatedly adding more detail to an algorithm until it is complete is called stepwise refinement. Stepwise refinement makes it possible for the programmer to concentrate on one small step at a time and thus avoid making the mistakes caused by attempting to consider too many details simultaneously.

How could you begin to put stepwise refinement into practice? Here are some suggestions.

(a)   Start with the output required from the program.
(b)   Proceed in SMALL steps, successively adding more detail.
(c)   Give a step that requires more detail a descriptive label, underline it, and then expand it into more detail at a later stage in the algorithm development.
(d)   Avoid the temptation to start at the beginning with the details of opening files, initialising variables, etc, — because at the beginning of the design phase, it is not always clear which variables are to be initialised, and which files are to be opened.
(e)   The algorithm you end up with need not be so detailed that each statement translates into one statement of coding, but it should not be so brief that essential points of logic are omitted, or that references to important procedures are left out.
(f)   If you cannot explain a step in structured English, explain it in ordinary English and then describe it in structured English.

Designing algorithms is an important part of any project or examination question which involves writing substantial programs.

12.5 SOLVING A PROGRAMMING PROBLEM

In general, a solution to a non-trivial programming problem should comprise

> algorithms
> data structure specifications
> program code
> further documentation

12.5.1 ALGORITHMS

The algorithm should be specified in a way which does not depend on any programming language. Structured English is suitable for specifying algorithms.

The algorithm should clearly show the necessary logic and procedures to solve the problem. It should be complete in all important respects.

The algorithm should be in outline or summary form. But the algorithm should not be so brief that a programmer (i.e. one of your contemporaries or class mates) would find it difficult to code (i.e. write the program) directly from it, or that an examiner could not easily determine whether the program code follows the algorithm structure.

Extensive validation should not be included — unless the question specifically requires it. Validation should not be ignored either — it should be discussed in the section on documentation.

In solving a programming problem, you are usually expected to demonstrate your problem solving and solution planning skills. A problem solving method for designing algorithms is stepwise refinement.

12.5.2 DATA STRUCTURES

Data structures should be defined and explained in a way which is independent of any programming language. Diagrams supported by explanations in English would be appropriate. Data structures include file organisation and record layouts, input data formats, output data formats and printlines, screens for interactive input and output, report formats and paging, and data structures such as arrays, stacks and queues. Examples of how data structures may be specified occur throughout this book.

The data structures should, of course, be appropriate to the problem, and be correctly defined and used within the program.

12.5.3 CODING

The program coding in the PROCEDURE DIVISION should clearly follow the given algorithm. The coding should also be syntactically correct, and be easy for an examiner to read and understand.

12.5.4 DOCUMENTATION

Documentation should include problem analysis (e.g. to produce . . . . from . . . .), test plans, operator or user instructions, and any other item which will add to the solution without repeating what has already been stated. Into this category might come mathematical formulae, worked examples and a discussion of problem solution strategy. Limitations, such as lack of validation, should be discussed.

Exercise 12.1

1 A serial file of the former students of a college is maintained for use when publicity is required for various fund raising activities. It has been decided to purge the file of all those records predating 1915 on the assumption that those former students are no longer active. The names and details of those students removed from the file are to be listed for reference and the remaining records written to two serial files, one for male students and one for female students.
(a) Design and write the program which will purge the file and produce the listing.
(b) Design your own record formats to include the following

     (i)   name
     (ii)   sex
     (iii)   date of leaving
     (iv)   qualification
     (v)   address

City and Guilds 1984

Note: 'produce the listing' means produce a report, with appropriate titles, headings and paging.

2 To make up the pay packets of the employees of a large factory it is necessary to perform a cash analysis. The denominations of the currency are notes to the value of 10, 5 and 1 pounds, and coins to the value of 50p, 20p, 10p, 5p, 2p, 1p, where 1 pound = 100p.
Design and write a program to accept the employee number and net wage and to tabulate, for each employee, his number, net wage, and the number of notes and coins of each denomination to make up his net wage. Also to calculate the total quantity for each denomination and the total money to be collected from the bank.

City and Guilds 1984

Note: 'tabulate' means produce a table. The table in this case would cover several pages (how many employees are there in a large factory?). Therefore paging, appropriate headings, page and report totals are required. An appropriate method of input would be from a file and not from the keyboard. Why?

3 Write an efficient routine which will search a table of data held in main store. Each line of the table contains an item code and its associated price. The table is in ascending order of the item code. Each item code appears in the table once only. Given an item code the routine should find and display the price of the item. If the item code is not contained in the table, a relevant message should be displayed.

City and Guilds 1983

Note: A linear search is not an efficient search routine. This, together with the information that the item codes are in ascending order and that none are duplicated, suggests that a logarithmic search (binary chop) would be appropriate. The table to be searched already exists in memory. How many entries are there in the table? How could your routine be used with tables of varying sizes? Could a value held in TABLE-SIZE be passed to your routine?

4 Write a program which will enable a doctor to retrieve information from a file of patients' records held on a direct access medium. The items in each record of the patients' file will be:

Reference number	8 alphanumeric
Surname	20 alphabetic
Initials	4 alphabetic
National health no.	10 alphanumeric
Allergies	20 digits
(up to 10 codes	
2 digits each)	
Diseases	20 digits
(up to 10 codes	
2 digits each)	

You should design your own file structure and specify the format for request of details and the displayed reply.

City and Guilds 1983

Note: How is a doctor going to identify the patient and retrieve the appropriate record? Is it reasonable for a patient, especially a very old one, to remember a reference number? What if a doctor wanted to look at Mrs Smith's record? Would a doctor know the correct reference number? Would a doctor necessarily want to see the whole of a patient's record? And would a doctor remember the meaning of each disease code? Would simple card indexes be useful?

5 A library maintains an indexed sequential file of members who are currently borrowing books. The file is sequenced and indexed on book accession number. Each record consists of borrower number, book accession number, title and date due back.
(a) Design and write a program which, given today's date and the accession number of the book, updates the file when a book is returned, and calculates the fine due at 1p for each day the book is overdue.
(b) Design your own record and field formats.

City and Guilds 1984

Note: A book accession number uniquely identifies each book. For example, if there were five copies of Computer Studies for A-level by T.A. Smith, then each copy would have a different accession number. Would you need to input a date every time a borrower returned a book? Would you need to input the borrower's number for each book returned at the same time by the same borrower?

6 Write a subroutine to validate the modulus 11 check digit of a 6 digit reference number, then write a simple program to test the subroutine. Provide a set of suitable test data.

The check digit will have been calculated as follows (using the number 224487 as an example).

Multiply each digit by its associated weight 7, 6, 5, 4, 3 and 2 and sum the results.
i.e. $2 \times 7 + 2 \times 6 + 4 \times 5 + 4 \times 4 + 8 \times 3 + 7 \times 2 = 100$

Divide by the modulus 11 giving a remainder of 1 which is then subtracted from the modulus 11 to give the check digit value of 10. The value of the check digit will be represented by the digits 1 to 9, T and E.

Thus the check 'digit' T would be appended to the reference number giving 224487T.

City and Guilds 1983

7 A boat hire company offers four kinds of boats for rental during the holiday season. The boats differ only in their size and the number of berths they have, that is, the number of people the boats can accommodate.

The four kinds of boat are rated 4, 6, 8 and 10 berth. A boat may be hired at a daily rate for any number of days. Alternatively the boats may be hired at the weekly rate for holidays which are multiples of 7 days. A holiday for a number of days not a multiple of 7 days will be charged at the weekly rate for complete weeks plus the daily rate for each additional day. Thus a 10-day holiday would be charged at ONE weekly rate plus THREE daily rates.

The company requires TWO tables to be produced
(a) listing the total charge for a holiday in EACH type of boat for a specified number of days in the format shown in Fig. 1 below
(b) similarly listing the cost of a berth to EACH individual member of a group assuming all berths are taken.

Fig. 1

Hire period in days	Number of berths			
	4	6	8	10
1				
2				
3				
4				
5				
6				
7				
10				
14				
28				

Design and write a program which would fulfil these requirements for the company.
City and Guilds 1985

8   A text file is held on a serial access medium. The file is to be edited by inserting, deleting and replacing complete lines of text. Each line of text consists of a 5 digit line sequence number and 40 characters of text. There may be unallocated line sequence numbers. Write a program for a text editor with the following specification. Lines of text, in the same format as the text file, are to be accepted from a terminal. If the line sequence number already exists in the text file, it is assumed to be a replacement line unless the text part of the input line is blank, in which case the line in the text file is deleted. If the line sequence number does not already exist in the text file it is assumed to be an insertion line.

The lines input from the terminal should be in sequence, but if an out of sequence line be entered a message is generated and the line is ignored. Line sequence number 99999 can be used to signal no more editing.

City and Guilds 1983

13
Data Flow Diagrams

13.1 INTRODUCTION

In practice, computer programs form only a small part of a data processing system. Computerised data processing systems involve both computer procedures and clerical procedures. These procedures usually process data. This chapter is about analysing and describing the flow of data from process to process in a data processing system. A theatre ticket reservation system is used to illustrate the principles.

13.2 CASE STUDY

The Marston Down Theatre Company presents four plays each year. Each play runs for five days — one performance per day. Tickets for each play are sold at the various shops in the region which act as the Company's agents. Each agent has a terminal linked to the theatre's computer. Each terminal comprises a VDU, keyboard and printer.

When a customer makes an enquiry about whether a ticket is available for the performance on a particular day, the agent, via the terminal, accesses the theatre's bookings file to determine which seats are not booked.

If the customer wishes to reserve a seat, the agent confirms the booking via the terminal (thus ensuring that the seat cannot be booked by anybody else). A ticket is then completed by the printer. The agent authenticates the ticket by putting the agency stamp on it, and then hands the ticket to the customer.

A reservation may be cancelled at any time up to the day before the performance. Customers who cancel receive a refund of 80% of the ticket price.

At the theatre, the bookings file is archived daily by copying it to a new file. Also, the computer is used to prepare and print, each week, a report on how well the tickets for the play are selling.

When a play has completed its run, a new bookings file for the next play is created.

13.3 DATA FLOW DIAGRAMS

We begin by considering the second paragraph of the case study: 'When a customer makes an enquiry about whether a ticket is available for the performance on a particular day, the agent, via the terminal, accesses the theatre's bookings file to determine which seats are not booked.' This process is shown in Figure 13.1

This diagram shows the essential elements of a data flow diagram. The curved arrows represent the flow of data. Each arrow has a label which describes the nature of the data. For example, available-seats represents a list of seats from which the customer can choose.

Straight lines represent a file. A file is not necessarily a computer file. It could be a book detailing money received. Or it could be a collection of ticket stubs stuck on a spike.

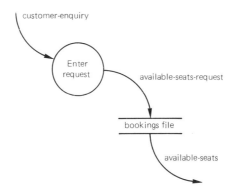

Figure 13.1

The bubble represents a process. Processes act on data. The data item 'customer wants to know whether there is a seat available on a particular day' is processed by the agent keying in the request in an appropriate form. This request for information on the availability of seats is processed by the computer.

Not all of the processes need be shown explicitly. In our example, file processing by computer is implied, as are validation and security processes. The amount of detail shown in a data flow diagram depends on its purpose. Our present purpose is to outline the important ponts of the theatre ticket reservation system.

Next, we consider the flow of data which leads to the production of a ticket. 'If the customer wishes to reserve a seat, the agent confirms the booking via the terminal (thus ensuring that the seat cannot be booked by anybody else). A ticket is then completed by the printer. The agent authenticates the ticket by putting the agency stamp on it, and then hands the ticket to the customer.' This process is shown in Figure 13.2

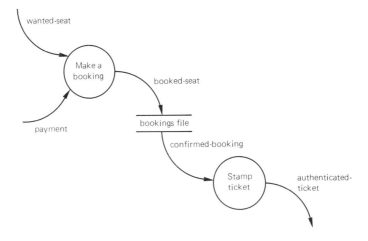

Figure 13.2

Now we look at the cancellation process. 'A reservation may be cancelled at any time up to the day before the performance. Customers who cancel receive a refund of 80% of the ticket price.' See Figure 13.3

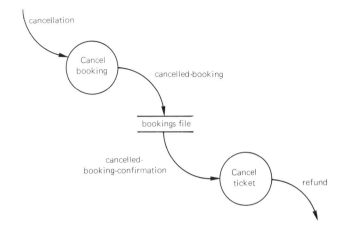

Figure 13.3

'At the theatre, the bookings file is archived daily by copying it to a new file. Also, the computer is used to prepare and print, each week, a report on how well tickets for the play are selling.' This process is shown in Figure 13.4.

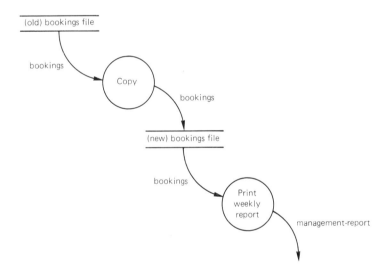

Figure 13.4

The next data flow diagram (Figure 13.5) shows the main parts of the theatre ticket booking system. The file creation and archiving procedures are not shown, nor are the accounting procedures.

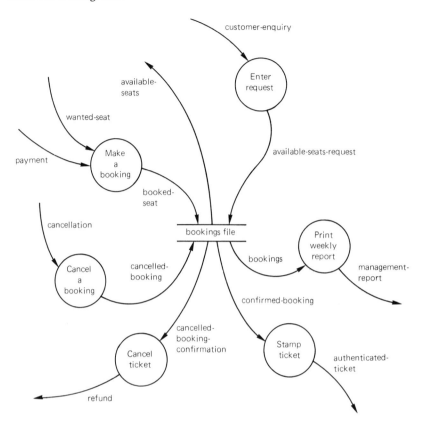

Figure 13.5. Data flow diagram for theatre seat reservations.

13.4 DATA DICTIONARY

Having considered the flow of data, we now consider the data itself. For each item of data, we mention its composition together with any other details, such as screen or printer formats, which might help to clarify its nature.

customer-enquiry
    made by telephone or in person
    whether seats are available for the current play on a particular day

available-seats-request
    entered at a terminal by the agent
    comprises
        agent identification code
        request for a particular day's seating plan

available-seats
    screen display showing a seating plan together with the seats that
        are available

wanted-seat
    entered by the agent
    comprises
        day code
        row number
        seat number

booked-seat
    entered by the agent
    comprises
        agent identification code
        booking request code
        day code
        row number
        seat number

confirmed-booking
    output by the computer
    comprises
        agent identification code
        booking confirmed message
        day code
        row number
        seat number

authenticated ticket
    output on card by printer
    comprises
        name of play
        location of play
        date and time of performance
        seat number
        agent stamp

bookings file	organisation indexed sequential
booking record	
seat number	key
day code	1 to 5
row	1 to 12
seat	1 to 16
status	booked or not booked
price code	A for seats in rows 3 to 6
	B for rows 7 to 10
	C for rows 1, 2, 11 and 12

A collection of details about data items such as the one shown above is called a data dictionary. A data dictionary helps clarify the data flow diagram by defining further the data involved. The construction of a data dictionary is extremely useful in the analysis and in the design of a data processing system.

13.5 HOW TO CONSTRUCT DATA FLOW DIAGRAMS

Data flow diagrams are easy to understand, but constructing them requires practice. Here are some suggestions on how to go about drawing data flow diagrams.

Do not expect to draw a perfect diagram at the first attempt. It is far easier to improve on something you have already drawn than it is to create a perfect diagram at the first attempt. Repeatedly improve and redraw your diagram.

Concentrate on the flow of data rather than on the processes. Label each data flow as you draw it. Give each data flow a name which describes its purpose. A data name should be meaningful to the intended reader.

Label the processes after the data flows have been labelled. The name to give a process should suggest itself from the data flowing into and out of the process.

If you find that your diagram is becoming uncomfortably crowded, combine several processes into one overall process in a main diagram. Then supplement your main diagram with a separate diagram on a fresh sheet in which this overall process is expanded into its constituent parts.

Aim for a consistent level of detail on any one page.

13.6 USES OF DATA FLOW DIAGRAMS

Data flow diagrams are used for analysing data processing situations, for designing new systems and for communicating system design features to other people.

Exercise 13.1

For each of the following system descriptions construct a data flow diagram and a data dictionary.

1 Stock control

Every month the technician of a college computer section determines how much paper is in stock for each of the section's various printers. By doing so, the rate at which the paper is being used can be measured. If it seems likely that the stock of a particular size of paper will not last the year, the technician estimates how much more paper will be required and informs the head of section.

The section head consults a list of outstanding orders (to ensure that the paper is not already on order), and the current balance of the section's consumables account (to check whether money is available for the purchase of more paper). If the head decides that more paper should be bought, the technician is asked to order some more. The order details are placed in the outstanding orders book.

When the paper arrives, the order is removed from the outstanding orders book.

2 Taxi business — private hire

Prospective clients enquire, by telephone or in person, whether a taxi is available to transport them to their destination. The taxi proprietor determines whether a taxi could be available at the right time and place. If the proprietor agrees to accept the business, the following items are recorded on a numbered form:

> client's name and the number of people to be transported
> place and time the client is to be picked up
> client's destination
> time the request for a taxi was made
> fare to be charged

About ten minutes before the taxi is due to collect the client (or earlier if the client is not local) the proprietor assigns the appropriate vehicle (four, six or twelve seats) and records, on the client's form, the driver and vehicle assigned to the client. The proprietor then notifies the driver, in person or by radio, about the client's requirements.

At a convenient moment, the proprietor transfers the form to a file.

At the appointed time, the taxi driver collects and transports the client to the destination, where the taxi driver is paid the required fare. If the client cannot be found at the rendezvous, or if the client flees from the taxi without paying, the driver informs the proprietor by radio. The proprietor makes an appropriate entry on the form.

The taxi business also has contracts with local firms and with the local education authority to transport people on a regular basis. For example, one contract may be to convey children between home and school every day during term time. Such clients are invoiced at the end of the month.

When the taxi driver finishes the shift, the driver returns to the proprietor and hands over the money that has been collected. The proprietor checks this amount against what should have been collected, refunds the driver for any money spent on fuel, and records the taxi's mileage and fuel purchased.

The proprietor pays casual drivers at the end of the shift and full time drivers at the end of the week. In both cases, the drivers are paid 30% of the cash value of the work they have done.

3 Holiday boat hire company

The Thames Narrow Boat Hire Company has seven bases on various canals throughout the country. Each base has a terminal comprising VDU, keyboard and printer. Each terminal is linked to the computer at the main base in Leicester. The computer is used for keeping track of the bookings for each boat, and for maintaining customer accounts.

Customers may take a boat from one base and return it to any other base.

There are two, three, four, six and eight berth boats available for hire. Periods of hire start on a Saturday between 3.00 and 5.30p.m. and finish on a Saturday at 9.00 a.m.

The hire charges depend upon:

> the size of boat (i.e. number of berths);
> the number of extra passengers (e.g. a two-berth boat may carry three people
>   altogether i.e. one extra passenger);
> the period of hire.

The following table gives an example of how the charges for a two berth boat vary with the period of hire.

Month	:	Mar	Apr	May	Jun	Jul	Aug	Sep	Oct
Charge per week	:	150	230	230	260	300	330	220	160

The charge per week includes VAT, diesel fuel, calor gas and toilet pump-out fees.

The customer chooses a boat from the catalogue and determines whether it is available for hire by telephoning any base. If it is available, the boat is 'held' for seven days.

A boat is 'booked' when the company receives a completed and signed booking form, with 20% (to the nearest pound) of the total hire charge, and an acknowledgement is sent to the customer.

Five weeks before the hire date, the customer is sent an invoice and asked to pay the balance of the hire charge at least three weeks in advance of the hire date.

After the boat has been returned, a damage refund cheque is sent to the customer — unless the boat was returned late, damaged or dirty. The customer is also re-imbursed for certain expenses during the hire period (e.g. for toilet pump-outs, fuel purchases, etc.).

Since each base performs a similar function to every other base, you need consider only one of them.

4   Printer quotations and work

(a)   A small printing firm provides quotations on request. The designer estimates the time that needs to be spent on the artwork by looking at past similar jobs. Details of these jobs are held in a filing cabinet in customer name order. The firm charges ten pounds per hour for artwork.

The designer then looks into a file detailing suppliers of paper and prices and decides whether it is more economical to buy paper already cut to the right size, or to buy larger, cheaper sheets. With paper that is too big, the most efficient way of dividing it up i.e. with the minimum of waste, would have to be devised, and the cost of the time that would be needed to cut the paper up would have to be calculated. The Paper Suppliers file is organised in supplier name order, and is updated at the beginning of each week by the designer telephoning the various suppliers and asking them for their latest prices.

The designer estimates the cost of materials and the time involved in making a printing plate, and the cost of the inks and the time involved in printing and finishing the job e.g. cutting, folding and stapling. The firm charges five pounds per hour for labour.

Finally, the designer forwards a copy of the quotation to the potential customer, and files a copy in the Quotations File.

(b)   A customer instructs the printing company to go ahead, as per quotation.

A job card is prepared from the quotation. The job card informs the employees of the customer's requirements. As each stage of the job is completed, details of the actual time spent, and the actual quantities of the various materials used, are recorded on the job card.

The completed job card is compared with the quotation to determine how accurate the estimate was, and these, together with the drawings, are filed in customer name order in the filing cabinet. The printing plates are also filled in customer name order: these are used for repeat orders.

The completed job is sent to the customer, together with an invoice requesting payment.

14

System Flowcharts

14.1 INTRODUCTION

A computer is usually not the only part of a data processing system. For example, in a computerised mail order system, clerks process customers' orders, warehouse staff pick goods from the shelves, despatch clerks pack goods, and accounts clerks process payments.

The flow of data from process to process, from department to department, or from person to person is outlined in a system flowchart — see Figure 14.1

14.2 ORDER PROCESSING

Figure 14.1 shows part of the order processing system for the Next Day Computer Supplies Company. The rectangles represent processes, the parallelograms represent documents or displays, and the open-headed arrows represent data entering or leaving the system as defined by the flowchart. The blacked-in arrows represent the flow of data or documents.

A customer chooses goods from a catalogue, and makes an order either by telephone or by post. Ordering by post involves filling in a form or writing a letter.

The order department clerks receive the customer's order. First, the clerks check whether the customer has an account with the company. If the customer is a new one, a new account is created, otherwise the account is checked to see whether the customer's credit limit is about to be exceeded. If the customer has insufficient credit, a credit review request is forwarded to the accounts department and the order is put to one side pending their decision.

Then the order department clerks check whether the goods are in stock. If an item is not in stock, the customer is informed and invited to either cancel the item from the order or to wait for the item to be despatched when the company receives fresh supplies. The order is then entered into the computer. The computer updates both the customer's account and the stock file, and prints several copies of the order.

One copy of the order, the picking note, is used by the warehouse staff to locate and select the items which make up the order. Details of these items are entered into the computer to confirm that the items have been physically removed from stock. Then, the warehouse staff forward the goods together with a copy of the order, called the advice note, to the despatch department. And they send another copy of the order, the invoice, to the accounts department.

The despatch department clerks pack the advice note with the goods before sending them by post, rail, road or air to the customer.

The accounts department clerks enter details of the order into the computer to check whether the customer's account has been updated correctly. Then the invoice is sent to the customer. The invoice instructs the customer on the amount and method of payment.

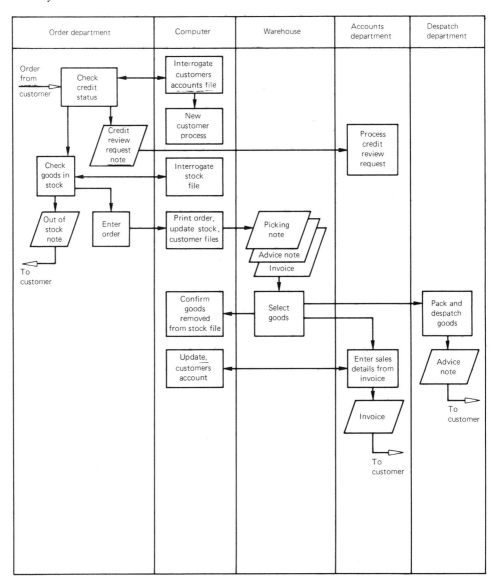

Figure 14.1   System flowchart for processing an order

14.3 SYSTEM FLOWCHARTS

System flowcharts are organised in columns. Each column is headed with the name of a department, person or function. System flowcharts show the flow of data from process to process, and the department or person or function responsible for each event. The system flowchart outlines the important events in a system.

Systems usually exist within the context of a network of systems. For example, the stock control system and the credit control system are linked to the customer order processing system to form a description of the company's business.

A process in a system flowchart can be expanded into more detail. Conversely, the processes in a system flowchart can be collected together and be represented as a single process in a larger system or network of systems.

System flowcharts are used for designing or for describing data processing systems.

14.4 DRAWING SYSTEM FLOWCHARTS

System flowcharts are easy to follow and understand, but constructing them requires practice. Here are some suggestions.

Carefully analyse the data processing system, e.g. by drawing data flow diagrams or rough system flowchart sketches, or by writing down the main points.

Identify the main processes/people/departments/functions involved and consider providing a column for each.

Sketch in the flow of data between the columns. Aim to arrange the flow, in general, from top to bottom, and from left to right. Try to avoid crossing data flow lines because crossed flow lines obscure clarity. Use rectangles to represent processes and parallelograms to represent documents or displays. Draw them freehand for the rough sketches, then use a flowchart template for the final neat version.

Make sure all the outputs and inputs to the system are accounted for.

Do not expect to get the system flowchart right first time. It is far easier to improve on something you have already drawn than it is to produce the perfect diagram first time. Repeatedly improve and redraw your diagram, with constant reference to the system description, adding more detail and rearranging the symbols as required.

If you find that your diagram is becoming uncomfortably crowded, combine some of the processes into one, and expand this process on another page. Do not continue a diagram onto the next page.

Aim for a consistent level of detail on any one page.

Practise.

Example

A hospital records system has been set up to deal with in-patient records for a busy city hospital. On-line access to patient records is available from terminals situated in the wards. The data displayed is limited to recent treatment and personal details. A more detailed printed record for a patient may be requested from a terminal in a ward. Update of the treatment details is usually done from the wards. Notification of discharge of patients may be done from a ward terminal or by an official form which is sent to the records department for transcription.

Admission of a patient may be performed from the casualty department terminal, but only if the record of that patient already exists, otherwise a detailed document must be completed and sent to the records department.

Scheduled admissions may be notified from the ward terminal on the assumption that a detailed record has already been produced from a form completed by a consultant.

City and Guilds 1985

The key departments or people involved seem to be the wards, the records department, the casualty department, the consultant. We provide a column for each. Since all the wards perform the same task, we can represent their function as one ward.

We look at the first five lines of the system description and focus our attention on ' . . . access to patient records . . . from terminals in the wards . . . more detailed printed record . . . may be requested . . . '. Straight away we see that a column for computer processing is required. We add it to our system flowchart, then sketch in the request for access to a patient's record (Figure 14.2a).

Now we consider 'Update of the treatment is usually done from the wards'. This is easily added to our sketch. The word 'usually' gives us a little concern for it implies that there could be exceptions. Who else could reasonably update the treatment details? The consultant? More likely the consultant's handwritten notes would be entered by the ward staff. The casualty department? Only if the record already exists. We add these points to our diagram (Figure 14.2b).

'Notification of discharge of patients may be done from a ward terminal or by an official form which is sent to the records department for transription'. When a patient is discharged, we do not want to lose the treatment record. Nor do we want it cluttering up the treatment file. So we copy it to an archive file before deleting it from the treatment file (Figure 14.2c).

'Admission of a patient from . . . the casualty department terminal, but only if . . . record exists, otherwise . . . document sent to records department' (Figure 14.2d).

Finally, we turn our attention to 'Scheduled admissions . . . from a ward terminal . . . form completed by consultant'. We include these points (Figure 14.2e).

Easy!

There is not one absolutely correct system flowchart for this medical records system. Versions which differ in detail but are still complete in all important respects are equally correct.

Exercise 14.1

1(a)   Read through the hospital records system description sentence by sentence and include any points that have been omitted from Figure 14.2. Include any other points not mentioned in the system description but which you think are important. These ponts should not conflict with those already described.

1(b)   Decide how the layout of the diagram could be improved. Would the diagram be clearer if the computer column came between the ward and records department? Could symbols be rearranged so that the flow is always from top to bottom and from left to right? Could the use of the symbols be more economical? For example, could the two admission procedures be linked by sharing their common processes? Refine, improve and redraw the system flowchart for the hospital records system (Figure 14.2).

14.5 ORGANISATION AND CONTENT OF FILES

System flowcharts by themselves are not very useful unless they are supported by, among other things, a description of the organisation and content of the main files involved. The hospital records system described in Section 14.4 suggests that the main files involved are a password file, a current patients treatment file, a current patients details file and an archive file of past patients. Some of the important details of these files are shown below.

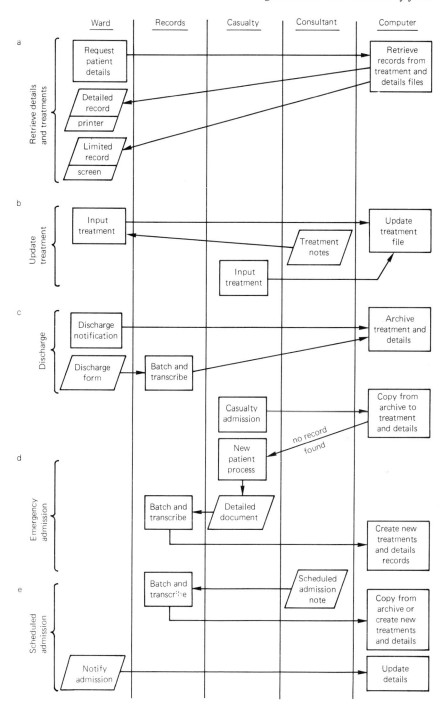

Figure 14.2   Construction of a hospital records system flowchart

password file	organisation direct access
password record	one record per authorised user
user-id	key
access level	e.g. to patient details only, or to details and treatment

The user enters their password before each access is made to a patient's record

current patients treatment file	organisation indexed sequential
treatment record	one record per treatment
patient-id	key
name	
sex	
date of birth	
general practitioner	
consultant	
ailment	includes consultants notes
treatment	includes date of treatment

current patients details file	organisation indexed sequential
patient record	one record per patient
patient-identifier	key
name	
sex	
date of birth	
address	
ward	
patient-id	pointer to treatment file

past patients file	organisation indexed sequential
past patient record	one record per patient
patient-id	key
general practitioner	
dates	repeated as required
date-discharged	
date-admitted	
treatment	repeated as required
ailment	
treatment	
consultant	

14.6 SYSTEM FLOWCHART EXAMINATION QUESTIONS

Exam questions that require a system flowchart to be drawn from a given system description are set by many examination boards. In general, an answer should comprise

(a)   a system flowchart to be produced from the system description
(b)   a description of the organisation and content of the main files involved
(c)   a description of the system. This may be directed (e.g. "Describe the security requirements") or more general (e.g. "Describe the system"). The narrative should provide further explanation of aspects of the system that are not clear from the system flowchart.

One problem that you may have with examination questions of this type is lack of time. Therefore, you should practise answering systems questions.

Exercise 14.2

1   Student applications processing

For the following system
   (a) draw an overall systems flowchart
   (b) give an example of the interactive dialogue which could occur in establishing an enquiry record.

A college student record system has been computerised and integrated into a comprehensive information system. The system operates on two files: an enquiry file and a master student file. When a student makes an enquiry about a course, a record is created on the enquiry file. Such enquiries are made by telephone, by post or by personal visit. In the first case, a clerk completes a form ready for processing, in the second case, a form is sent to a prospective student and in the third case information is entered by means of an interactive terminal. The enquiries are processed automatically and decisions on admittance are reported.

The student must then apply for admittance and this causes a transfer of the record to the master file, if the application is in agreement with the admittance decision. The creation of a master record is reported to the head of an appropriate department, the college registrar and the student. This record acts as a receipt for the student's payment of fees which must be submitted with the application. The admittance report includes details of the appropriate fees.

If an enquiry does not provide adequate information for an automatic decision, the enquiry is reported to the academic department which follows it up and subsequently updates the record or deletes it. A monthly report of the enquiries and admittances is produced.

City and Guilds 1977

2   Credit card accounting

Draw an overall system flowchart for the following system and indicate the layout and content of the master file(s) which would need to be maintained.

A credit card company uses a computer system to maintain the accounts of its customers. When a customer uses his credit card to make a purchase a voucher is sent by the shopkeeper to the computer centre. The voucher is machine-readable and is used to adjust the accounts of both customer and shopkeeper. Every month the shopkeeper receives a payment covering the amount owing to him: cheques for this are printed by the computer. Every month the customer receives a statement indicating what he owes the credit card company: he can pay anything between 10% and 100% of this amount, interest being charged monthly on the outstanding balance. His payment is accompanied by a form from which information is punched and input to the computer to update his account. An on-line enquiry facility is provided so that checks may quickly be made to see whether a customer has reached his credit limit.

City and Guilds 1980

3   Estate agents

Draw system flowchart(s) and describe the following system. Your answer must include details of the organisation and content of the files which would be needed.

The system is for use by a firm of estate agents, who require a computer-based system to maintain a file of the properties which they have for sale, in order to send details of suitable properties to clients on their mailing list, and also provide information retrieval in their offices for enquirers who call in person.

There are five offices, one of which acts as the main office and coordinates the functions of itself and the other four. The computer is housed in the main office, and every office (including the main office) has a terminal on-line to the computer. The terminal facilities consist of VDU, keyboard and letter quality printer. At the main office the computer has disk storage on which the property file and customers' requirements are stored.

Prospective clients are likely to call, in person, at any office and describe their requirements. The counter staff will feed these requirements into the computer via the terminal and receive a list of suitable properties displayed on the VDU with optional hard-copy from the printer.

It is likely that such customers will ask to be placed on the mailing list, in which case either the requirements already fed in can be used, or else they can fill in a form, from which the office staff subsequently input details via the terminal keyboard. Mailing list letters, with details of suitable properties pulled off the file in accordance with the customer's stored requirements, are printed by the computer at the main office and sent out, once per week. Every four weeks a form is sent out inviting the customer to indicate whether he or she wishes to remain on the mailing list. If the reply is no, then the customer's record is deleted; alternatively, the customer has the opportunity to amend details of his or her record.

Whenever a new property is added to the agent's books, details of this must be input on-line by the branch office concerned, to up-date the property file. Other updates to the property file, again initiated at an office and input on-line, are amendments to details held (such as change of price), and inputs to state that:

(a) the property is under offer (it remains on file until sold);

(b) the sale of the property is completed (the record is then deleted).

Details of properties sold are transferred to a history file, from which monthly and annual sales reports are produced.

The prospective customer's requirements, which have been stored and matched against appropriate fields on the property file, are:

> Price range (minimum/maximum)
> Number of bedrooms (minimum/maximum)
> Geographical area (up to four different areas)
> Is garage required? (no, 1 car, 2 cars, more than 2 cars)
> Is garden required? (no, small, medium, large)
> Customer's name, address and telephone number will also be stored.

City and Guilds 1985

4   Employment agency

Draw system flowcharts to define the system described below. Supplement your charts by writing a description of the system, covering such points as validation, file organisation and security.

SYSTEM DESCRIPTION

This is a system to be run at an employment agency, to match people seeking jobs to suitable job vacancies. Clients have personal details and information about their experience and qualifications stored on file, and wish to receive details of vacancies for which they may be suitable.

There are two parts to the system: the first, which uses batch processing, is run weekly. Under this part of the system clients automatically receive notification of suitable vacancies. You must describe how your system ensures that, having once been notified of a vacancy, a client is not repeatedly notified of the same vacancy on subsequent runs. There is also an on-line part of the system, whereby clients may visit the employment agency and be shown details of vacancies on a VDU, with the option of a hard-copy print-out of vacancies which are of interest.

The system must provide for:

(a) updating the client file with
     (i)   new client information
     (ii) amendments to existing client information
     (iii) deletion of client record, either on request or because client's subscription period has expired.
(b) updating the vacancies file with
     (i)   new vacancies
     (ii) amendments to existing vacancies
     (iii) deletion of vacancies.

Information input to the update procedure must be suitably validated. During update, all client's records must be checked for expiry of subscription period: in these cases a letter is printed inviting the client to renew.

City and Guilds 1983

5   Car hire firm

Design a system in outline to satisfy the following requirements.

A car hire firm operates a self-drive service from 30 offices throughout the UK, most of them being at airports or main railway stations. Customers may pick up a car at one office and return it to the company at a different office.

At the company's London headquarters is a large computer supporting terminals in each of the offices. Each office terminal consists of a VDU, keyboard and hard-copy printer.

You are to design a system to run on this computer configuration to satisfy the following requirements.

Customers may book cars for hire by telephone, by letter or by calling in person. These booking requests should be addressed at least 3 days in advance to the office where the customer wishes to pick up the car. Since cars may be hired from one office and returned to another, the computer must keep track of the location of each car and what bookings are arranged for it. A minimum of 8 hours is required between bookings for any one car, for maintenance. Each car is serviced every 5000 miles, so the computer must keep details of mileages for each car. If an office does not have enough cars at a particular time to cover its bookings then customers are turned away.

OUTPUTS required at each office are

1) A twice-daily print-out showing the bookings so far recorded for that office for the next 72 hours. (Details of which cars are booked and which cars are due for service.)
2) Details of each car can be displayed on the VDU on request, showing current bookings on file, present location, mileage since last service.
3) Computer-printed confirmation of booking is produced and posted first-class to telephone or postal customers and handed to personal callers.

INPUTS (via the keyboard) at each office are
1) Bookings. The clerk inputs the date and time of collection, date, time and place of returning, size of car required.
2) Collection. Hirers pay a deposit on collecting the car. The clerk inputs details of this and confirms to the system that the car is now out on hire.
3) Return. Hirers pay the balance of the hire charge on return. The clerk inputs details of this and the car mileage.

Your answer should consist of two parts.
(a) Indicate the content and layout of the master file(s) which you consider would be needed to operate this system. (List the items of data which you would choose to store and give the size and data type of each item.)
(b) Draw a system flowchart to illustrate your proposed system. Since all the offices perform identical functions it is only necessary to show one of them in detail.

City and Guilds 1982

6   Examinations

Draw an overall system flowchart for the following system and describe briefly the main programs which would be needed.

Music examinations are held at different centres all over the country but are coordinated by an Examination Board in London. There are 30 examiners and 200 centres, which are usually schools. At the beginning of the year the centres provide the Board with a list of dates within the relevant period on which they can be used for examinations. Examinations are arranged to take place over a 3-week period and applications to take the examinations have to be sent to the Board at least 2 months before the beginning of this period. The application states the name and address of the candidate, the grade of the examination and the musical instrument concerned. The appropriate fee has to be sent with the application. The system is required to produce the following outputs:
(a) an acknowledgement to the applicant of the receipt of the application and fee
(b) a letter to each applicant informing him or her of the date and time of the examination, the address of the centre and the name of the examiner
(c) a master schedule giving full details of the arrangements for each centre
(d) a list for each centre giving the schedule for that centre (this is an individual section of (c) above)
(e) a list for each examiner giving details of the candidates he or she is to examine and the dates, times and centres at which the examinations are to be held.

City and Guilds 1981

7   Holiday bookings

Draw system flowchart(s) for the following system and indicate the content of the files which would be used.

C & G Holidays are a package holiday firm who arrange holidays at 30 hotels in Mediterranean holiday resorts. Holiday bookings come from travel agents, and also directly from the public, and can be made by telephone, by post, or by calling in person at any one of 10 C & G offices, situated within a 50 mile radius of the company's headquarters in London. Most people call in person at a travel agent, but the agent contacts C & G by telephone, so these count as telephone bookings. Postal enquirers are sent a booking form to fill in and return, or they can use the form which is printed in the company's brochure; personal callers fill in the form at the C & G office, and telephone bookings have to be followed up by a written confirmation within 7 working days otherwise the booking lapses. Booking forms and the written confirmation which follows a telephone booking have to be accompanied by a deposit (or the full amount if booking is made less than 4 weeks before the departure date). No booking is accepted (except telephone bookings pending receipt of confirmation) without deposit or full payment).

The 'package' includes airline tickets, so at the time of booking the C & G clerk contacts the airline by telephone to reserve the seats, and this again is followed up by a form, sent by a courier after the customer's deposit has been received, to confirm the airline booking.

C & G send notification of booking to the hotel, and when acknowledgement is received from both airline and hotel, C & G send a confirmation of booking to the customer. Four weeks before the departure date the balance of the holiday price has to be paid, so one week prior to this C & G send a reminder to the customer. (This does not apply in the case of holidays booked less than four weeks before departure, which have to be paid for in full at the time of booking.) Two weeks before departure date (and only if the holiday has been fully paid for) the airline tickets and vouchers for the hotel rooms are sent to the customer, together with a questionnaire which the customer is invited to return after the holiday giving comments and suggestions. C & G compile a digest of these suggestions for circulation among the management.

Computing facilities are as follows: each of the 10 C & G offices has a large micro system consisting of processor, with disk drives and line printer, and VDU/ keyboards at the office counter. A customer file is kept on disk at each office, and each office deals with its own customers. Thus, letters are generated and sent out by an office, hotel vouchers and airline tickets are printed by the office, which then sends them to the customer. At the same time, each office computer is on-line to the mainframe computer at C & G's headquarters, and it is here that a central file of hotel accommodation is maintained on disk.

City and Guilds 1984

15
Modular Programming

15.1 INTRODUCTION

Small programs have important advantages over large ones: they are easier to design, test, understand and modify. And because small programs are simpler than large ones, they are more likely to be free from errors.

A small program is one which is easily managed. Its ideal size depends upon the complexity of the task. The more complex the task, the smaller the program should be. Up to about 120 lines (two pages) of coding is easily managed by most programmers, and is, therefore, a reasonable maximum to aim at. This maximum can be increased if the program remains easy to understand and modify.

Unfortunately, small programs may only be used to carry out small tasks. However, many small programs can be organised and linked together so that large scale data processing tasks may be accomplished.

15.2 DUPLICATING PROGRAM CODE

If we have three programs, one to create a file, one to output that file's records on the printer, and one to retrieve information from the file, then all three programs would share the same file structure. This means that the code describing the file in each program would be identical.

Having duplicate program code is, a potential source of error. For example, if the file structure in one program was changed, then the file structure in all of the others would have to be changed also. If by some oversight the three copies of the file definition were not identical, unexpected results will occur. The possibility of this happening is removed if there is only one copy of the file definition. The COPY statement makes this possible.

Suppose the following COBOL file description was held in a disk file called FILEDESC.COB.

```
FD F1-SUBS-FILE
    LABEL RECORDS ARE STANDARD
    VALUE OF FILE-ID IS "SUBS.DAT".
01  F1-SUBS-REC.
    05  F1-NAME      PIC X(20).
    05  F1-ADDRESS   PIC X(50).
```

Then this could be incorporated in any program by writing

```
COPY FILEDESC.COB.
```

in the FILE SECTION

For example

```
* { This file creation program uses the COPY statement to }
* { include the file description in the coding.           }
      IDENTIFICATION DIVISION.
      PROGRAM-ID.   TM151.
      ENVIRONMENT DIVISION.
      INPUT-OUTPUT SECTION.
      FILE-CONTROL.
            SELECT F1-SUBS-FILE
               ASSIGN TO DISK.

      DATA DIVISION.
      FILE SECTION.
      COPY FILEDESC.COB.

      PROCEDURE DIVISION.
      010-CONTROL.
            OPEN OUTPUT F1-SUBS-FILE
            DISPLAY "To end file creation, enter *** for name"
            DISPLAY "Name?"
            ACCEPT F1-NAME
            PERFORM 020-LOOP UNTIL (F1-NAME = "***")
            GO TO 030-CLOSE.
      020-LOOP.
            DISPLAY "Address?"
            ACCEPT F1-ADDRESS
            WRITE F1-SUBS-REC
            DISPLAY "Name?"
            ACCEPT F1-NAME.
      030-CLOSE.
            CLOSE F1-SUBS-FILE
            STOP RUN.
```

The contents of FILEDESC.COB are included by the compiler when the COPY command is translated.

Exercise 15.1

1   A file contains the following fields: name, address and telephone number. Design and write three programs, one to create the file, one to display the file contents and one to display the corresponding address and telephone number when given a name. The File Definition should be held on disk and be included in the programs by using the COPY statement. A portion of program code which can be used by several programs is called a library.

15.3 CALLING PROGRAMS

In this section we see how several programs can work together as a single unit.

In the following structured English algorithm, <u>create</u> creates a file, <u>print</u> displays the records of the file on the printer, and <u>search</u> is a simple file search.

```
menu
     done ← false
     while (done = false) do
          display menu
          input choice
          if (choice = e) then
          done ← true
          else if (choice = c) then
               create
          else if (choice = p) then
               print
          else if (choice = s) then
               search
          else
               error in choice
     endif
     endwhile
     stop
```

Translating this algorithm into COBOL we obtain:

```
*  ( This program passes control to other programs by CALLing
*  ( them.

   IDENTIFICATION DIVISION.
   PROGRAM-ID.   MENU.
   ENVIRONMENT DIVISION.
   DATA DIVISION.
   WORKING-STORAGE SECTION.
   01   W-CHOICE    PIC X.
   01   W-DONE      PIC X(5).

   PROCEDURE DIVISION.
   010-CONTROL.
        MOVE "FALSE" TO W-DONE
        PERFORM 020-MENU UNTIL (W-DONE = "TRUE")
        GO TO 030-END.

   020-MENU.
        DISPLAY "Menu: C(reate, P(rint, S(earch, E(xit: "
        ACCEPT W-CHOICE
        IF (W-CHOICE = "E" OR "e")
             MOVE "TRUE" TO W-DONE
        ELSE IF (W-CHOICE = "C" OR "c")
             CALL "CREATE"
        ELSE IF (W-CHOICE = "P" OR "p")
             CALL "PRINT"
        ELSE IF (W-CHOICE = "S" OR "s")
             CALL "SEARCH"
        ELSE
             DISPLAY W-CHOICE " NOT UNDERSTOOD".

   030-END.
        STOP RUN.
```

The program displays a simple menu. If the user enters C for example, then control is passed to a program whose PROGRAM-IDentity is CREATE. This program is shown below.

```
* This program is CALLed by the menu program.  It displays
* a message on the screen, and then returns control to the
* menu program.
 IDENTIFICATION DIVISION.
 PROGRAM-ID.  CREATE.
 ENVIRONMENT DIVISION.
 DATA DIVISION.
 PROCEDURE DIVISION USING.
 010.
      DISPLAY "File CREATION program called".
 020.
      EXIT PROGRAM.
```

The file creation does not actually take place at the moment. The details of the file creation can be included in this program skeleton or stub at a later date.

The PROGRAM-IDentity should begin with a letter. Only the first six characters are taken notice of by the compiler, i.e. are significant. This means that the first six characters in the PROGRAM-IDentity of any CALLed program should be different from the PROGRAM-IDentity of any other CALLed program.

The PROCEDURE DIVISION heading in a CALLed program should include the word USING.

EXIT PROGRAM should appear in a paragraph by itself. Its effect is to return control to the CALLing program, to the statement following the CALL command. The CALL statement can be thought of as meaning 'go there, do it then come back', just like with the PERFORM command.

A CALLed program can be designed and tested in isolation, i.e. without reference to any other program by leaving out the phrase USING and writing STOP RUN instead of EXIT PROGRAM. Then when the program is working satisfactorily, it can be incorporated in a larger program. Thus, a large program can be made up of many proven programs.

Exercise 15.2

1 Enter and compile the four programs, Menu, Create, Print and Search, as mentioned in Section 15.3 above. Print and Search are identical to Create, except for the message each outputs. Link the four programs together by using a link/loader such as microsoft's L80. Use a command line something like:

```
TM152/N,TM152,TM153,TM154,TM155/G
```

where the items following the /N symbol, TM152, TM153, TM154, and TM155 represent the program names you used when editing and compiling the four programs. The four programs are consolidated by L80 into one executable program represented by TM152.COM. If you are not using Microsoft software, consult the appendix and your manuals.

15.4 LOCAL AND GLOBAL VARIABLES

The values of data items can be changed only by the program in which the data items were declared, i.e. data cannot be transferred between programs — unless the contrary is specified. For example:

```
* { This program passes a data value to the program it CALLs
  IDENTIFICATION DIVISION.
  PROGRAM-ID.  MAINPROG.
  ENVIRONMENT DIVISION.
  DATA DIVISION.
  WORKING-STORAGE SECTION.
  01  W-NAME     PIC X(20).
  01  W-NUMBER   PIC X(4).
  PROCEDURE DIVISION.
  010.
      DISPLAY "Name?"
      ACCEPT W-NAME
      DISPLAY "Number?"
      ACCEPT W-NUMBER
      CALL "SUBPROG" USING W-NUMBER
      STOP RUN.



* { This program displays a data value passed to it by the }
* { CALLing program                                        }
  IDENTIFICATION DIVISION.
  PROGRAM-ID.  SUBPROG.
  ENVIRONMENT DIVISION.
  DATA DIVISION.
  WORKING-STORAGE SECTION.
  01  W-NAME     PIC X(20).

  LINKAGE SECTION.
  01  L-NUMBER  PIC X(4).

  PROCEDURE DIVISION USING L-NUMBER.
  010.
      DISPLAY "Name: " W-NAME
      DISPLAY "Number: " L-NUMBER.
  020.
      EXIT PROGRAM.
```

Program 1 invites the user to enter a name followed by a number. Program 2 displays the number typed in because its value is transferred from program 1. But for the name, it displays just the heading "Name": U.C.N: because the value of W-NAME is not transferred.

Variables to be shared are specified in the CALLing program and in the CALLed program. In the CALLing program, they are declared in the WORKING-STORAGE SECTION and listed in the CALL statement USING list. In the CALLed program, they are listed in the LINKAGE SECTION and in the PROCEDURE DIVISION USING list. The order in which the variables are specified in the CALL USING and in the PROCEDURE DIVISION USING lists must match, but they need not have the same names.

The variables can be referred to by a group name. For example, in the CALLing program we might write:

```
*  ( This program passes data by group name )
   IDENTIFICATION DIVISION.
   PROGRAM-ID.   MAINPROG.
   ENVIRONMENT DIVISION.
   DATA DIVISION.
   WORKING-STORAGE SECTION.
   01   W-CLIENT.
        05   W-REF-NUMBER   PIC X(6).
        05   W-NAME         PIC X(20).
        05   W-ADDRESS      PIC X(50).
   PROCEDURE DIVISION.
   010.
        MOVE "1" TO W-REF-NUMBER
        MOVE "FRED" TO W-NAME
        MOVE "UNKNOWN" TO W-ADDRESS
        CALL "SUBPROG" USING W-CLIENT
        STOP RUN.
```

And in the CALLed program:

```
*  ( This program receives data by group name )
   IDENTIFICATION DIVISION.
   PROGRAM-ID.   SUBPROG.
   ENVIRONMENT DIVISION.
   DATA DIVISION.
   LINKAGE SECTION.
   01   L-CLIENT.
        05   L-REF-NUMBER   PIC X(6).
        05   L-NAME         PIC X(20).
        05   L-ADDRESS      PIC X(50).
   PROCEDURE DIVISION USING L-CLIENT.
   010.
        DISPLAY L-CLIENT.
   020.
        EXIT PROGRAM.
```

Where several programs share the same variable, it is possible for one program to change the value of the data item without any adverse affect on itself, but with a disastrous affect on the performance of another program. Therefore programs which are part of a larger program should be designed to work as independently as possible.

A variable whose value can be altered only by the program in which it is declared is called a local variable. A global variable is one whose value can be altered by several programs.

It is easy to remember where the LINKAGE SECTION comes in the DATA DIVISION: FOWLS — FILE SECTION, WORKING-STORAGE SECTION, LINKAGE SECTION and (if your compiler supports it) SCREEN SECTION.

15.5 COMPUTER RUNCHARTS

Suppose a sequential file of amendments to a payroll master file is to be created, and that this file is to be used to update the sequential master file. How could we start designing the necessary programs? We could start by listing the main processes involved.

```
create amendment file and validate batch totals
validate the amendments
sort the validated amendments file to payroll file sequence
update the payroll file
```

Since these processes occur in a predictable order, (for example, creation, and validation will always occur before sorting takes place — the computer operator cannot specify otherwise) we can represent them on a computer runchart — see Figure 15.1. A computer runchart always has five columns headed input files, master files, processes, other file and output files. It shows the relationship between the processes and the inputs, files and outputs.

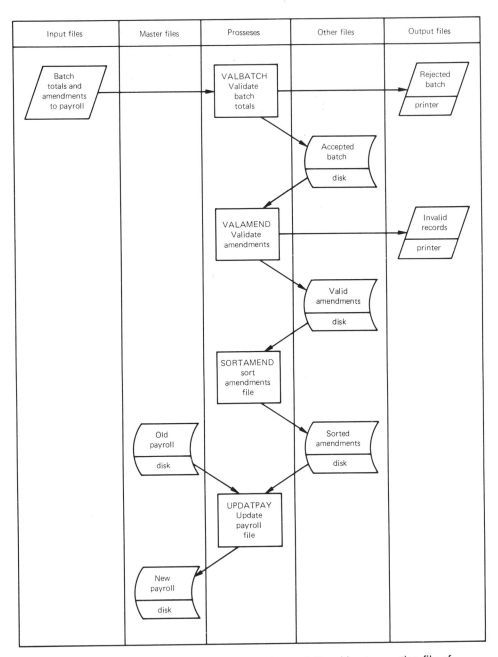

Figure 15.1 Computer Runchart showing update of payroll file with a transaction file of amendments

The batch totals and the amendments are input to the batch validate program — VALBATCH. If the totals computed by the program do not match those input, then details of the rejected batch are output to the printer; otherwise the file of amendments — the accepted batch — is output to disk.

This file is then used as input to the next program, VALAMEND, which validates the amendments, checking that the contents of each field conform to specification. Invalid records are output to the printer, whereas valid records are output to another disk file.

This file of valid amendments is then used as input to the SORTAMEND program. The output of this program is a sorted file of validated amendments.

This sorted file of amendments, together with the current generation of the master payroll file, is used as input to the update program, UPDATPAY. The output from the update program is the new generation of the master payroll file.

In practice, dumps of the various files would be output to the printer for visual inspection. These are called proof lists. They are not shown in Figure 15.1, but they could be included in a computer runchart.

The program which controls VALBATCH, VALAMEND, SORTAMEND and UPDATPAY is not shown on the runchart. Its PROCEDURE DIVISION comprises a sequence of CALL statements.

```
PROCEDURE DIVISION.
010.
    CALL "VALBATCH"
    CALL "VALAMEND"
    CALL "SORTAMEND"
    CALL "UPDATPAY"
    STOP RUN.
```

15.6 PROGRAM STRUCTURE CHARTS

A program which is CALLed can itself CALL other programs. A program structure chart is a convenient way of showing such a hierarchy — see Figure 15.2.

The STARTUP-SHUTDOWN program passes control to the MENU program. Depending on the user's choice, this program either returns control to STARTUP-SHUTDOWN or passes control to CREATE-FILE or to UPDATE. UPDATE gets from the user the key value of the record to be amended, inserted or deleted. If this value is invalid, then control returns to MENU, otherwise control passes to SEARCH. Depending upon the result of the search, control passes either to the DELETE-AMEND program (key found in file) or to the INSERT program (key not found in file). Either way, control returns to MENU via SEARCH and UPDATE.

While a program structure chart is useful for showing the hierarchical structure within a program, it does not reveal anything about the logic involved.

Programs which are part of a larger program are often called sub-programs. Other names for sub-programs are routines, modules, procedures or functions. Whatever they are called, they usually carry out some well defined task.

The rectangle symbol in a program structure chart represents a module. Depending on the level of detail, a module could represent a program, a section in a COBOL program, a group of paragraphs or just a paragraph.

Exercise 15.3

1 The Marston Down Theatre Company presents four plays each year. Each play runs for five days — one performance per day. Tickets for each play are sold at the various shops in the region which act as the Company's agents. Each agent has a

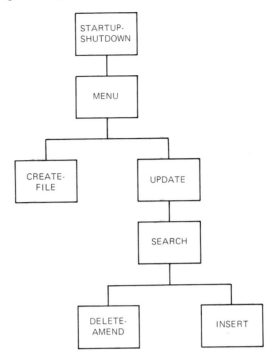

Figure 15.2 Program structure chart showing the hierarchy of modules

terminal linked to the Theatre's computer. Each terminal comprises a VDU, keyboard and printer.

When a customer makes an enquiry about whether a ticket is available for the performance on a particular day, the agent, via his terminal, accesses the Theatre's Bookings File to determine which seats are not booked.

If the customer wishes to reserve a seat, the agent confirms the booking via his terminal (thus ensuring that the seat cannot be booked by anybody else). A ticket is then completed by the printer. The agent authenticates the ticket by putting his stamp on it, and then hands the ticket to the customer. The agent marks the booked seat on his hard copy of the seating plan.

A customer may cancel his reservation at any time up to the day before the performance. Customers who cancel receive a refund of 80% of the ticket price.

At the Theatre, the Bookings File is archived daily by copying it to a new file. Also, the computer is used to prepare and print, each week, a report on how well tickets for the play are selling.

When a play has completed its run, a new Bookings File for the next play is created.
The Bookings File comprises:

```
Booking record
    seat number
        day code      (1 to 5)
        row           (1 to 12)
        seat          (1 to 16)
    status            (booked or not booked)
    price code        (A : 5 pounds for seats in rows 3 to 6
                       B : 3 pounds for rows 7 to 10
                       C : 1 pound for rows 1, 2, 11 and 12)
```

The Management Report contains:
> the number of seats unsold for each price category;
> the total value of sales to date.

(a) Draw a system flowchart for this theatre seat reservation system.
(b) Design, write and test separate programs (modules) to:
    (i) create the Bookings File
    (ii) produce a seating plan on the screen, together with an indication of which seats are booked
    (iii) update the Bookings File whenever a booking or cancellation is made
    (iv) print the Management Report
    (v) archive the Bookings File.
(c) Design and write a control module to execute the modules (i), (ii), (iii), (iv) and (v) specified above. Since the order in which these modules are to be executed cannot be predicted, e.g. the Management Report is not necessarily printed after each update, the control module should provide a suitable menu. The control module should be tested before the other modules are linked with it.
(d) If your computer is a multi-user system (i.e. one which provides file and record locking — to prevent two users simultaneously updating the same record) then make your programs capable of supporting several simultaneous users. Ensure that only the master user is allowed to create a new file, print the Management Report and archive the Bookings File.

2 A film and video hire company wishes to computerise its loans system.

Hirers pay a yearly subscription which entitles them to borrow up to three items at a time. In addition, they pay a daily rate or a weekly rate for each item they borrow. A day is reckoned to be 24 hours from the time of hire.

Hirers choose the item they want from a catalogue, and, if the item is available, it is booked out to them. If the item is already out on hire, then hirers have the option of reserving it.

Hirers are sent reminders when an item is overdue. Hirers are also sent invitations to renew their subscription one month before it is due to lapse.

Every month, the company produces a catalogue of its current stock.

Design a computerised loans system for this company. Your design should include:
(a) a system flowchart;
(b) details of the organisation and content of files;
(c) a description of recovery procedures in case of data loss or corruption;
(d) an account of security considerations;
(e) printer formats;
(f) prototype programs to help the company finalise its requirements and approve the interface between the programs and the company's staff.

3 Design and implement a computerised dating agency.

16
Project Work

16.1 INTRODUCTION

Substantial, non-trivial programming projects are required in computing courses such as City and Guilds 418 and GCE A-level Computing Science. Usually, such a project should be fully documented. Ideas for projects may be found in Chapter 13 (Data Flow Diagrams), Chapter 14 (System Flowcharts) and in Chapter 15 (Modular Programming).

16.2 PROJECT DOCUMENTATION

The purpose of project documentation is to communicate the nature and substance of your project to the examiner, who is going to assess it. Your project is evaluated entirely on the basis of what you present. Good presentation creates a favourable impression. Use the following points as a guide when writing up your project.

PRESENTATION
Your project should be typed (use a word processor) on A4 or standard listing paper (approximately eight and a half by eleven inches) and presented in a lightweight cover. There should be no loose sheets of paper. Use a flowchart template with a sharp pencil or a fine black or blue ball-point or roller-point pen. Avoid using coloured inks or crayons, even for the title page.

TITLE PAGE
The first page should comprise your project title, your name and course, the date, and any other details required by the examination board, such as centre and candidate numbers.

CONTENTS
The second page should list the contents of your project report together with page numbers.

SUMMARY
No more than half a side of A4 should be devoted to a summary of your project. The summary should cover the main points and be on its own page.

INTRODUCTION
The scope of your project is defined in this section:

the task you set yourself (e.g. to computerise the scheduling of competitors in the Charles Keene Horse Trials Competition.);

the main methods used to accomplish the task (e.g. ascertain the current manual system by questioning and watching the horse trials organiser at work, devise appropriate data structures, design, write and test programs to assign starting times to competitors.);

the relevant background to the project (e.g. each horse competes in three events; dressage, show jumping and cross country. Only one horse at a time is in the dressage ring and in the show jump arena. Horses start the cross country course at two minute intervals. At least half an hour must elapse from the time a rider completes one event, e.g. show jumping, before starting in the next event, e.g. cross country.)

limitations and constraints (e.g. the project does not include scoring procedures. A computer with twin 400K floppy disk drives is used. This limits the maximum number of competitors to two hundred and fifty.);

your specific aims (e.g. to maintain a list of registered competitors; to produce lists of competitors in (a) rider name order, (b) horse name order, (c) start time order, for each of the three events.)

Of course, you would include more detail than is shown here.

The level of detail you should aim at is one which would enable a student on your course, who knows nothing about your work, to easily understand and extend your project. You should avoid repeating yourself. You should also write concisely by including only the words and facts that are essential.

SYSTEM DESCRIPTION
This section should include data flow diagrams (Chapter 13), system flowcharts (Chapter 14) and, if appropriate, computer runcharts (Chapter 15). The charts should be suppported by a detailed written description of the data processing system.

PROGRAM DOCUMENTATION
The data dictionary (Chapter 13) should record the main data structures used, such as file and record structures (Chapters 5, 8, and 9 to 11) report formats (Chapter 6) and input/output screen formats (Chapter 7).

Then, for each program in turn, appropriate entries under the following headings should be included.

purpose	— a one sentence description of the purpose of the program
usage	— how the program is invoked or CALLed
example	— of one program run, to help the user establish whether the program is installed correctly
algorithm	— an outline of the program structure in structured English (Chapters 1 and 12). Hierarchical program structure charts could be included at this point (Chapter 15)
limitations	— bugs which have been deliberately left in the program, such as lack of validation
listing	— the program error listing, as output from the compiler. This could be held in an appendix or in a separate folder
test runs	— the results of executing your program with the test data specified in your test plan (Chapter 4)
dumps	— of files before and after their contents are changed. These should be annotated by hand.

How should program listings be documented? Who reads your program listings? You do, and so do other programmers. You may need to read your program listings a long time after the program was created and its details forgotten — perhaps to amend it, or to remind yourself about a particular technique, or to make use of it in another program. Other programmers will read your program listings if they are investigating the reasons why it does not work as it should, or if they are checking it for correctness, or if they are amending it to perform a different function. If others do not find your coding easy to follow and understand, then the process of checking or amending it will be unnecessarily hard and liable to produce errors. In industry, about 80% of programmer effort is spent amending previously written programs. This is called program maintenance or enhancement. A program which is easy to read and understand is easy to maintain. An easily maintained program is an efficient program in the sense that it is easily changed to meet new requirements with minimum programmer effort. Some features which help make a program maintainable are:

structure — for example, a program which follows a clearly defined algorithm specified in structured English

layout — which corresponds to the conventions of structured English with good use of indentation

data names — which are comprehensible, informative and descriptive, for files, records, data items, screens, paragraphs, sections and programs

comments — of explanation within the coding. These should improve the readability of the coding. They should not be so detailed that the flow of logic is obscured, nor should they be so sparse that difficult or complex algorithms remain obscure to the reader. Comments should not be written by hand as an after-thought. (Think how many times you might amend a program in the course of its lifetime.)

Program documentation is for the benefit of those programmers who need to inspect the coding. What about the people who just want to use the program? Program users are not necessarily programmers. So they should not be expected to read program listings.

USER AND OPERATOR DOCUMENTATION
Some of the kinds of people who use programs are

yourself
other programmers
trained computer operators
people who have been trained to use a particular program
people with no knowledge of computing.

The success with which other people use your program depends on the quality of your instructions. Good user instructions are presented at a level appropriate to the understanding of the intended user. So, when designing user instructions, the first question to ask yourself is: who is going to use my program?

If the answer is 'a person with no specialist knowledge of computing', then a system of comprehensible prompts, menus and help files, written in English (not in programming jargon) and displayed on the screen would be appropriate. The amount of detail displayed should be chosen by the user so that, as the user's competence increases, the level of detailed help can be reduced. Too much help is as irritating as too little.

On the other hand, if the answer is 'a trained computer operator', and the program is the monthly payroll for a large firm for example, then information and prompts such as what program is running, when to load which disk drive with which file, when to change the paper on the printer, and reasons for program termination, such as run time error or successful conclusion, would be appropriate. Only minimal information should appear on the screen if a batch of data is being processed.

Good screen designs are not enough. They should be supplemented with well written manuals. How to write extensive instruction manuals is beyond the scope of this book. However, when designing written user instructions, the following items should be considered for inclusion.

1 a list of programs and files which should be present together with the disk drives which should be on-line
2 an indication of the disk space and memory requirements
3 the size, type and quantity of paper which should be mounted in the printer
4 instructions on how to load the program into memory
5 directions on how to abort program execution and how to restart it
6 a list of error messages which might be seen during program execution, and what to do about them
7 instructions on how to recover from mistakes
8 descriptions of what the program user will see
9 step by step instructions, at each stage, on what to do next

You should assume that the user knows how to use the computer: how to switch it on, boot the operating system, load disks, etc. What the user does not know is how to use your program. The program user certainly does not want to know how to edit, compile and link a program.

CONCLUSIONS
You should mention how well your project met your intentions, how your project could be improved and how your project could be extended.

APPENDICES
The final section should be your appendices. Here, you could include information, such as program listings and annotated file dumps, which would interrupt the flow of your presentation if included in the main body of your project write up.

Whether you omit some of these points, or include others to suit your particular project, your work should be fully documented.

16.3 CHOOSING A PROJECT

The subject of your project should be realistic. This does not mean that your suite of programs should be complete in itself. Rather, your programs could be part of a wider collection of programs, some of which you will not implement.

Try to obtain some experience of working in the chosen data processing system. But be warned that there is a risk of either being overwhelmed with a mass of information, or being rejected. Quite often, firms are too busy with their own problems, or are concerned with their own security, to be bothered by a student with a project to do.

Start with the design of a complete data processing system. Then narrow your interest down to a few well defined, well chosen data processing situations for which you have a chance of writing good programs in the time available. Projects nearly always take longer than you think they will. Use a variety of programming techniques and data structures.

Above all, enjoy your project.

Answers to Selected Exercises

Exercise 1.1

1 find-highest
      read first number
      highest-so-far ← number
      repeat 5 times
          read next number
          if (number > highest-so-far) then
            highest-so-far ← number
          endif
      endrepeat
      write out highest-so-far

2 state-of-account
      read money-in-account
      if (money-in-account < 0) then
          write "overdrawn"
      endif
      if (money-in-account = 0) then
          write "empty"
      endif
      if (money-in-account > 0) then
          write "in credit"
      endif

3 pounds-to-dollars
      read number-of-pounds
      number-of-dollars ← number-of-pounds × 1.50
      write number-of-dollars

4 count-names
      number-of-names <— 0
      read first name
      while (name not = ***) do
          add 1 to number-of-names
          read next name
      endwhile
      write number-of-names

5 print-results
read first name
while (name not = ***) do
　　　　　　read next mark
　　　　　　if (mark < 0) then
　　　　　　　　write "mark less than 0"
　　　　　　endif
　　　　　　if (mark >= 0 and < 40) then
　　　　　　　　write name, "fail"
　　　　　　endif
　　　　　　if (mark >= 40 and < 58) then
　　　　　　　　write name "pass"
　　　　　　endif
　　　　　　if (mark >= 58 and < 75) then
　　　　　　　　write name, "credit"
　　　　　　endif
　　　　　　if (mark >= 75 and < 100) then
　　　　　　　　write name, "distinction"
　　　　　　endif
　　　　　　if (mark > 100) then
　　　　　　　　write "mark more than 100"
　　　　　　endif

　　　　　　read next name
　　　　endwhile

Exercise 2.2

1

```
1.   *   ( This program displays whether a bank account is in credit
         IDENTIFICATION DIVISION.
         PROGRAM-ID.   TMA1.
         ENVIRONMENT DIVISION.
         DATA DIVISION.
         WORKING-STORAGE SECTION.
         01  W-MONEY-IN-BANK-ACCOUNT   PIC S9999.
         PROCEDURE DIVISION.
         PARAGRAPH-1.
             DISPLAY "Enter an amount of money - whole pounds only"
             ACCEPT W-MONEY-IN-BANK-ACCOUNT
             IF (W-MONEY-IN-BANK-ACCOUNT < 0)
                 DISPLAY "OVERDRAWN".
             IF (W-MONEY-IN-BANK-ACCOUNT = 0)
                 DISPLAY "ACCOUNT EMPTY".
             IF (W-MONEY-IN-BANK-ACCOUNT > 0)
                 DISPLAY "IN CREDIT".
             STOP RUN.
```

Exercise 2.3

1
```
      * ( This program counts names )
        IDENTIFICATION DIVISION.
        PROGRAM-ID.   TMA2.
        ENVIRONMENT DIVISION.
        DATA DIVISION.
        WORKING-STORAGE SECTION.
        01   W-NUMBER-OF-NAMES   PIC 999.
        01   W-NAME              PIC X(25).
        PROCEDURE DIVISION.
        010-LOOP-CONTROL.
            MOVE 0 TO W-NUMBER-OF-NAMES
            DISPLAY "Enter a list of names."
            DISPLAY "To end your list enter ***"
            DISPLAY "First name?"
            ACCEPT W-NAME
            PERFORM 020-LOOP UNTIL (W-NAME = "***")
            GO TO 030-NEXT-BIT.

        020-LOOP.
            ADD 1 TO W-NUMBER-OF-NAMES
            DISPLAY "Next name?"
            ACCEPT W-NAME.

        030-NEXT-BIT.
            DISPLAY "The number of names is " W-NUMBER-OF-NAMES
            STOP RUN.
```

Exercise 3.2

3
```
      * ( This program uses an array of names )
        IDENTIFICATION DIVISION.
        PROGRAM-ID.   TMA3.
        ENVIRONMENT DIVISION.
        DATA DIVISION.
        WORKING-STORAGE SECTION.
        01   W-LIST-OF-NAMES.
             02 W-NAME           PIC X(20)   OCCURS 10 TIMES.
        01   W-LISTSIZE          PIC 99      VALUE 10.
        01   W-POSITION          PIC 99.
        01   W-POSITION-OUT      PIC Z9.
        PROCEDURE DIVISION.
        010-INPUT-LOOP-CONTROL.
            MOVE 0 TO W-POSITION
            PERFORM 020-INPUT-LOOP W-LISTSIZE TIMES
            GO TO 030-OUTPUT-LOOP-CONTROL.
        020-INPUT-LOOP.
            ADD 1 TO W-POSITION
            DISPLAY "Name?"
            ACCEPT W-NAME (W-POSITION).

        030-OUTPUT-LOOP-CONTROL.
            MOVE 0 TO W-POSITION
            PERFORM 040-OUTPUT-LOOP W-LISTSIZE TIMES
            GO TO 050-DISPLAY-A-NAME.
        040-OUTPUT-LOOP.
            ADD 1 TO W-POSITION.
            MOVE W-POSITION TO W-POSITION-OUT
            DISPLAY W-POSITION-OUT, "   ", W-NAME (W-POSITION).

        050-DISPLAY-A-NAME.
            DISPLAY "Enter number corresponding to required name"
            ACCEPT W-POSITION
            DISPLAY W-NAME (W-POSITION)
            STOP RUN.
```

Exercise 3.3

2 To set up a table containing month names is straightforward. Declare

```
01   W-MONTH-NAMES.
     02   W-MONTH  PIC XXX   OCCURS 12 TIMES.
```

in WORKING-STORAGE, then in the PROCEDURE DIVISION write

```
MOVE "JAN" TO W-MONTH (1)
MOVE "FEB" TO W-MONTH (2)
MOVE "MAR" TO W-MONTH (3)
```

and so on. There is a more elegant way. Define the table of month names in WORKING-STORAGE thus.

```
01   W-MONTH-TABLE.
     02   W-MONTH-NAMES   PIC X(36)   VALUE
          "JANFEBMARAPRMAYJUNJULAUGSEPOCTNOVDEC".
```

We need to pick out groups of three letters for each month. So declare

```
01   W-MONTHS REDEFINES W-MONTH-TABLE.
     02   W-MONTH-NAME   PIC XXX OCCURS 12 TIMES.
```

The REDEFINES clause states that

```
02   W-MONTH-NAMES   PIC X(36)   VALUE
     "JANFEBMARAPRMAYJUNJULAUGSEPOCTNOVDEC".
```

and

```
02   W-MONTH-NAME   PIC XXX OCCURS 12 TIMES.
```

is one and the same object. So

```
W-MONTH-NAME (1) = "JAN"
W-MONTH-NAME (2) = "FEB"
W-MONTH-NAME (3) = "MAR"
```

and so on. COBOL does not allow us to use the VALUE clause and the OCCURS clause together in the same declaration.

```
*  { This program sets up a table of month names,  }
*  { inputs a month name from the user and outputs }
*  { the corresponding month number                }
   IDENTIFICATION DIVISION.
   PROGRAM-ID.  TMA4.
   ENVIRONMENT DIVISION.
   DATA DIVISION.
   WORKING-STORAGE SECTION.
   01  W-MONTH-TABLE.
       02  W-MONTH-NAMES    PIC X(36) VALUE
                            "JANFEBMARAPRMAYJUNJULAUGSEPOCTNOVDE
   01  W-MONTHS REDEFINES W-MONTH-TABLE.
       02  W-MONTH-NAME     PIC XXX   OCCURS 12 TIMES.
   01  W-MONTH-NUMBER       PIC 99.
   01  W-MONTH-IN           PIC XXX.
   PROCEDURE DIVISION.
   010-FILL-TABLE.
       DISPLAY "Month (JAN..DEC)?"
       ACCEPT W-MONTH-IN
       MOVE 1 TO W-MONTH-NUMBER
       PERFORM 020-SEARCH-TABLE UNTIL (W-MONTH-NUMBER > 12)
       STOP RUN.

   020-SEARCH-TABLE.
       IF (W-MONTH-IN NOT = W-MONTH-NAME (W-MONTH-NUMBER))
           ADD 1 TO W-MONTH-NUMBER
       ELSE
           DISPLAY "The month number is " W-MONTH-NUMBER
           MOVE 13 TO W-MONTH-NUMBER.
```

Exercise 6.2

1 (b)

```
BB-WRITE-AND-READ.
    IF (WD-EOP = "TRUE")
        WRITE PRINTLINE FROM WA-REPORT-HEADING
            AFTER ADVANCING PAGE
        WRITE PRINTLINE FROM WB-REPORT-COLUMNS
            AFTER ADVANCING 5 LINES
        MOVE SPACES TO PRINTLINE
        WRITE PRINTLINE AFTER ADVANCING 2 LINES
        ADD 1 TO WA-REPORT-PAGE
        MOVE "FALSE" TO WD-EOP.
    IF (F1-GRADE = "D" OR "C" OR "P")
        MOVE F1-NAME TO WC-REPORT-NAME
        MOVE F1-GRADE TO WC-REPORT-GRADE
        WRITE PRINTLINE FROM WC-REPORT-LINE
            AT END-OF-PAGE MOVE "TRUE" TO WD-EOP.
    READ F1-RESULTS-FILE
        AT END MOVE "TRUE" TO WD-EOP.
```

Exercise 9.1

1 (a) Writing the COBOL program from the structured English is quite straightforward. A little thought is required on how the key field number should be defined and how, for example, get-next-T should be written.

If number was defined as numeric (i.e. PIC 9s) we would need to make the declaration

```
01   W-HIGH-VALUE   PIC 9999   VALUE 9999.
```

and make it illegal for an employee to have 9999 as an employee-number. Since we do not intend to carry out arithmetic on number we could define it as an alphanumeric (i.e. PIC Xs) data item. Then we could use the COBOL pre-declared data item HIGH-VALUE (or HIGH-VALUES).

HIGH-VALUE is a COBOL defined constant whose value comes at the end of the ASCII collating sequence. In the ASCII collating sequence, the upper case characters (A, B, C, . . .) appear in alphabetical order, then a few symbols such as [\], then the lower case characters (a, b, c, . . .) in alphabetical order and finally a few more symbols such as {}˜. When sorting takes place, items are placed in order according to a collating sequence such as ASCII.

One way of translating

```
get-next-T
     if (not end-of-transaction-file) then
          retrieve next T
     else
          T ← HIGH-VALUE
     endif
```

```
GET-NEXT-TRANS-RECORD.
     IF (F2-TRANSACTION-KEY-KEY NOT = HIGH-VALUE)
          READ F2-TRANSACTION-FILE
               AT END MOVE HIGH-VALUE TO F2-TRANSACTION-KEY.
```

Here is the complete program.

```
* { This program updates a sequential master file with a }
* { sequential transaction file of amendments             }
  IDENTIFICATION DIVISION.
  PROGRAM-ID.   TMA5.
  ENVIRONMENT DIVISION.
  INPUT-OUTPUT SECTION.
  FILE-CONTROL.
       SELECT F1-MASTER-FILE ASSIGN TO DISK.
       SELECT F2-TRANSACTION-FILE ASSIGN TO DISK.
       SELECT F3-NEW-MASTER-FILE ASSIGN TO DISK.
```

```
DATA DIVISION.
FILE SECTION.
FD  F1-MASTER-FILE
     LABEL RECORDS ARE STANDARD
     VALUE OF FILE-ID IS "MASTER.DAT".
01  F1-MASTER-RECORD.
     05  F1-MASTER-KEY  PIC X(4).
     05  F1-NAME        PIC X(15).
     05  F1-DEPT        PIC X(10).
FD  F2-TRANSACTION-FILE
     LABEL RECORDS ARE STANDARD
     VALUE OF FILE-ID IS "TRANSACT.DAT".
01  F2-TRANSACTION-RECORD.
     05  F2-TRANSACTION-KEY  PIC X(4).
     05  F2-NAME             PIC X(15).
     05  F2-DEPT             PIC X(10).
     05  F2-UPDATE-TYPE      PIC X.
FD  F3-NEW-MASTER-FILE
     LABEL RECORDS ARE STANDARD
     VALUE OF FILE-ID IS "NEWMASTR.DAT".
01  F3-NEW-MASTER-RECORD.
     05  F3-NEW-MASTER-KEY  PIC X(4).
     05  F3-NAME            PIC X(15).
     05  F3-DEPT            PIC X(10).
PROCEDURE DIVISION.
AA-CONTROL.
     OPEN INPUT F1-MASTER-FILE
     OPEN INPUT F2-TRANSACTION-FILE
     OPEN OUTPUT F3-NEW-MASTER-FILE
     PERFORM EA-GET-NEXT-MASTER-RECORD
     PERFORM EB-GET-NEXT-TRANS-RECORD
     PERFORM BA-COMPARE-KEYS UNTIL (F1-MASTER-KEY = HIGH-VALUES
                          AND F2-TRANSACTION-KEY = HIGH-VALUES)
     CLOSE F1-MASTER-FILE
           F2-TRANSACTION-FILE
           F3-NEW-MASTER-FILE
     STOP RUN.


BA-COMPARE-KEYS.
     IF (F1-MASTER-KEY = F2-TRANSACTION-KEY)
        PERFORM CA-EQUAL-KEYS
     ELSE IF (F1-MASTER-KEY NOT = F2-TRANSACTION-KEY)
        PERFORM CB-UNEQUAL-KEYS
     ELSE
        DISPLAY "This should not happen!"
        STOP RUN.
```

```
CA-EQUAL-KEYS.
    IF (F2-UPDATE-TYPE = "A")
        PERFORM DA-AMEND
    ELSE IF (F2-UPDATE-TYPE = "D")
        PERFORM DB-DELETE
    ELSE
        DISPLAY "ERROR - equal keys and wrong update type!"
        STOP RUN.
CB-UNEQUAL-KEYS.
    IF (F2-TRANSACTION-KEY < F1-MASTER-KEY)
        PERFORM DC-INSERT
    ELSE IF (F2-TRANSACTION-KEY > F1-MASTER-KEY)
        PERFORM DD-WRITE-M-TO-NEW
    ELSE
        DISPLAY "This should not happen!"
        STOP RUN.

DA-AMEND.
    MOVE F2-TRANSACTION-KEY TO F3-NEW-MASTER-KEY
    MOVE F2-NAME TO F3-NAME
    MOVE F2-DEPT TO F3-DEPT
    WRITE F3-NEW-MASTER-RECORD
    PERFORM EA-GET-NEXT-MASTER-RECORD
    PERFORM EB-GET-NEXT-TRANS-RECORD.
DB-DELETE.
    PERFORM EA-GET-NEXT-MASTER-RECORD
    PERFORM EB-GET-NEXT-TRANS-RECORD.
DC-INSERT.
    MOVE F2-TRANSACTION-KEY TO F3-NEW-MASTER-KEY
    MOVE F2-NAME TO F3-NAME
    MOVE F2-DEPT TO F3-DEPT
    WRITE F3-NEW-MASTER-RECORD
    PERFORM EB-GET-NEXT-TRANS-RECORD.
DD-WRITE-M-TO-NEW.
    WRITE F3-NEW-MASTER-RECORD FROM F1-MASTER-RECORD
    PERFORM EA-GET-NEXT-MASTER-RECORD.

EA-GET-NEXT-MASTER-RECORD.
    IF (F1-MASTER-KEY NOT = HIGH-VALUE)
        READ F1-MASTER-FILE
            AT END MOVE HIGH-VALUE TO F1-MASTER-KEY.
EB-GET-NEXT-TRANS-RECORD.
    IF (F2-TRANSACTION-KEY NOT = HIGH-VALUE)
        READ F2-TRANSACTION-FILE
            AT END MOVE HIGH-VALUE TO F2-TRANSACTION-KEY.
```

Exercise 13.1

1

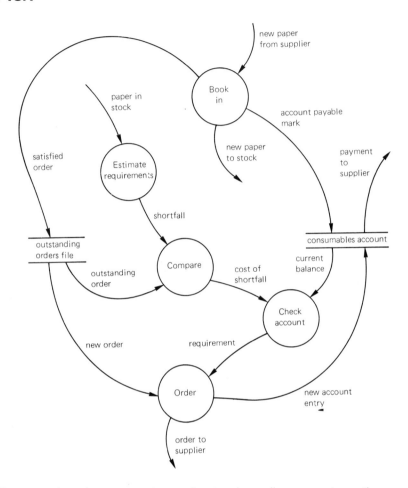

Data flow diagram to show the paper stock control system in a college computer section.

Exercise 14.2

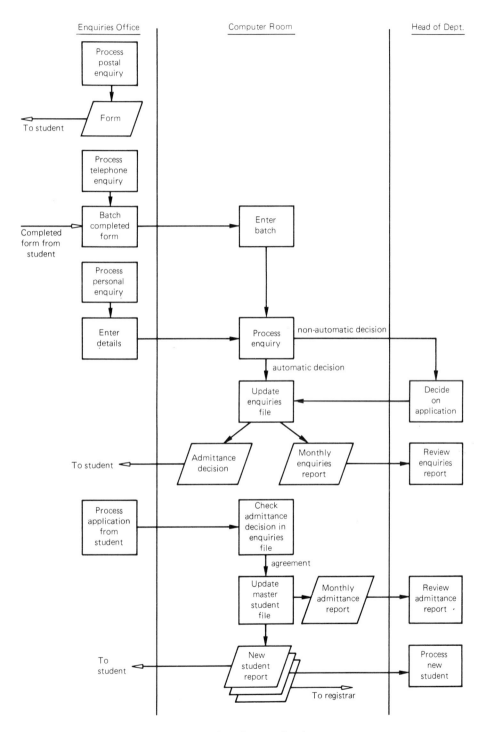

System flowchart to show the processing of student applications

Appendix

Micro Focus Level II COBOL Programs

1 INTRODUCTION

The programs contained in the main part of this book are written in Microsoft COBOL. The main difference between this COBOL and other COBOL implementations lies in the screen formatting statements. The programs in this appendix are written in Micro Focus COBOL and illustrate some of the differences between the two implementations of the language. If you are using Micro Focus COBOL, this appendix will help you to complete the exercises which can be found throughout the book.

2 THE FIRST ACCEPT STATEMENT

The Micro Focus COBOL compiler produces intermediate code which can be executed by the run time interpreter. To use the interpreter, a command line like

```
run programname
```

is entered. Depending on how your compiler has been configured, it is possible that the return signal, generated by pressing return after typing 'run programname', is passed to the first ACCEPT statement in your program. If program TM22 on page 12 does not wait for the user to enter a number to represent an examination mark, then make the declaration

```
01   W-JUNK      PIC X.
```

in WORKING-STORAGE (junk because the value it contains is to be junked and not used) and make

```
ACCEPT W-JUNK
```

the first statement in the PROCEDURE DIVISION, as shown in the following program.

```
*  { This program displays either 'pass' or 'fail' }
*  { Micro Focus COBOL version                     }
   IDENTIFICATION DIVISION.
   PROGRAM-ID.   TM22B.
   ENVIRONMENT DIVISION.
   WORKING-STORAGE SECTION.
   01   W-EXAM-MARK   PIC 999.
   01   W-JUNK          PIC X.
   PROCEDURE DIVISION.
   PARAGRAPH-1.
       ACCEPT W-JUNK
       DISPLAY "Please enter an exam mark"
       ACCEPT W-EXAM-MARK
       IF (W-EXAM-MARK < 40)
           DISPLAY "fail"
       ELSE
*          { exam-mark is 40 or more }
           DISPLAY "Pass".
       STOP RUN.
```

3 INITIALISING FIELDS

Suppose the variable W-NAME was defined to be

```
01   W-NAME                  PIC X(10).
```

and it held the value "TERRY". If the statement

```
ACCEPT W-NAME
```

was subsequently executed and "∗∗∗" was input, then W-NAME would have the value "∗∗∗RY". This would cause a problem if the execution of a loop depended on whether W-NAME = "∗∗∗", as in

```
PERFORM 020-LOOP UNTIL (W-NAME = "***")
```

A solution is to clear the data item of any none-space data value by executing

```
MOVE SPACES TO W-NAME
```

before executing

```
ACCEPT W-NAME
```

The following program illustrates the point.

```
* { This program counts the number of names in a list of names  }
* { Answer to Question 1 Exercise 2.4 Micro Focus COBOL version }
 IDENTIFICATION DIVISION.
 PROGRAM-ID.   TM24B.
 ENVIRONMENT DIVISION.
 WORKING-STORAGE SECTION.
 01   W-JUNK               PIC X.
 01   W-NUMBER-OF-NAMES    PIC 99.
 01   W-NAME               PIC X(10).
 PROCEDURE DIVISION.
 010-LOOP-CONTROL.
      ACCEPT W-JUNK
      MOVE 0 TO W-NUMBER-OF-NAMES
      MOVE SPACES TO W-NAME
      DISPLAY "Enter a list of names."
      DISPLAY "To end your list enter ***"
      ACCEPT W-NAME
      PERFORM 020-LOOP UNTIL (W-NAME = "***")
      GO TO 030-NEXT-BIT.
 020-LOOP.
      ADD 1 TO W-NUMBER-OF-NAMES
      MOVE SPACES TO W-NAME
      DISPLAY "Next name?"
      ACCEPT W-NAME.
 030-NEXT-BIT.
      DISPLAY "The number of names is " W-NUMBER-OF-NAMES
      STOP RUN.
```

4 FILES

In Micro Focus COBOL, the internal filename is connected with the external filename by the SELECT clause. For example

```
SELECT F1-MEMBERS-FILE ASSIGN TO "N:MEMBFILE.DAT".
```

assigns the filename used by the program, F1-MEMBERS-FILE, to the filename used by the operating system. The N: in "N:MEMBFILE.DAT" specifies that the file is held on disk drive N.

```
* { This program creates a file of subscribers to the }
* { Society for the protection of Small Mammals       }
* { Micro Focus COBOL version                          }
 IDENTIFICATION DIVISION.
 PROGRAM-ID.   TM51B.
 ENVIRONMENT DIVISION.
 INPUT-OUTPUT SECTION.
 FILE-CONTROL.
      SELECT F1-MEMBERS-FILE ASSIGN TO "N:MEMBFILE.DAT".
 DATA DIVISION.
 FILE SECTION.
 FD   F1-MEMBERS-FILE.
 01   F1-MEMBERS-RECORD.
      05   F1-NAME                 PIC X(20).
      05   F1-ADDRESS              PIC X(50).
      05   F1-CLASS-OF-MEMBERSHIP  PIC X.
 WORKING-STORAGE SECTION.
 01   W-JUNK                       PIC X.
```

```
PROCEDURE DIVISION.
010-CONTROL.
     ACCEPT W-JUNK
     OPEN OUTPUT F1-MEMBERS-FILE
     DISPLAY "Members file creation."
     DISPLAY "(To end the file creation enter *** for name)"
     MOVE SPACES TO F1-MEMBERS-RECORD
     DISPLAY "Name?"
     ACCEPT F1-NAME
     PERFORM 020-LOOP UNTIL (F1-NAME = "***")
     GO TO 030-CLOSE.
020-LOOP.
     DISPLAY "Address?"
     ACCEPT F1-ADDRESS
     DISPLAY "Class of membership?"
     ACCEPT F1-CLASS-OF-MEMBERSHIP
     WRITE F1-MEMBERS-RECORD
     MOVE SPACES TO F1-MEMBERS-RECORD
     DISPLAY "Name?"
     ACCEPT F1-NAME.
030-CLOSE.
     CLOSE F1-MEMBERS-FILE
     DISPLAY "End of members file creation."
     STOP RUN.
```

The next program retrieves records from a file. Notice that W-END-OF-FILE has two possible values: SPACES or TRUE.

```
*  ( This program displays the contents of the file of )
*  ( subscribers to the Society for the protection of   )
*  ( Small Mammals. Micro Focus COBOL version           )
   IDENTIFICATION DIVISION.
   PROGRAM-ID.   TM52B.
   ENVIRONMENT DIVISION.
   INPUT-OUTPUT SECTION.
   FILE-CONTROL.
        SELECT F1-MEMBERS-FILE ASSIGN TO "N:MEMBFILE.DAT".
   DATA DIVISION.
   FILE SECTION.
   FD   F1-MEMBERS-FILE.
   01   F1-MEMBERS-RECORD.
        05   F1-NAME                  PIC X(20).
        05   F1-ADDRESS               PIC X(50).
        05   F1-CLASS-OF-MEMBERSHIP   PIC X.
   WORKING-STORAGE SECTION.
   01   W-END-OF-FILE                 PIC X(5).
   PROCEDURE DIVISION.
   010-CONTROL.
        OPEN INPUT F1-MEMBERS-FILE
        DISPLAY "Members file"
        MOVE SPACES TO W-END-OF-FILE
        READ F1-MEMBERS-FILE
             AT END MOVE "TRUE" TO W-END-OF-FILE.
        PERFORM 020-LOOP UNTIL (W-END-OF-FILE = "TRUE")
        GO TO 030-CLOSE.
   020-LOOP.
        DISPLAY F1-MEMBERS-RECORD
        MOVE SPACES TO F1-MEMBERS-RECORD
        READ F1-MEMBERS-FILE
             AT END MOVE "TRUE" TO W-END-OF-FILE.
   030-CLOSE.
        CLOSE F1-MEMBERS-FILE
        DISPLAY "End of members file."
```

5 USING A NETWORK PRINTER

If your program accesses the printer directly, and if your computer is part of a network in which the printer is shared and output to it is queued i.e. spooled, network problems may arise. Programs which output to a shared network printer should direct the output to a file on disk instead. Then, on completion of program execution, the file can be output to the printer by using an operating system command such as PRINT filename.

The external filename could be given the extension .PRN to show that it is a PRiNter file.

```
*  { This program prints out a table of numbers,              }
*  { their squares and their cubes                            }
*  { Micro Focus COBOL and shared network printer version }
   IDENTIFICATION DIVISION.
   PROGRAM-ID.   TM61B.
   ENVIRONMENT DIVISION.
   INPUT-OUTPUT SECTION.
   FILE-CONTROL.
        SELECT PRINT-TABLE ASSIGN TO "PRINTAB.PRN".
   DATA DIVISION.
   FILE SECTION.
   FD PRINT-TABLE.
   01   PRINTLINE   PIC X(80).
   WORKING-STORAGE SECTION.
   01   W-COLUMN-HEADINGS.
        05   FILLER   PIC X(29)   VALUE SPACES.
        05   FILLER   PIC X(6)    VALUE "NUMBER".
        05   FILLER   PIC XX      VALUE SPACES.
        05   FILLER   PIC X(6)    VALUE "SQUARE".
        05   FILLER   PIC XXX     VALUE SPACES.
        05   FILLER   PIC X(4)    VALUE "CUBE".
        05   FILLER   PIC X(30)   VALUE SPACES.
   01   W2-REPORT-LINE.
        05   FILLER            PIC X(31)   VALUE SPACES.
        05   W2-NUMBER-OUT     PIC Z9.
        05   FILLER            PIC X(5)    VALUE SPACES.
        05   W2-SQUARE-OUT     PIC ZZ9.
        05   FILLER            PIC X(5)    VALUE SPACES.
        05   W2-CUBE-OUT       PIC ZZZ9.
        05   FILLER            PIC X(30)   VALUE SPACES.
   01   W3-NUMERIC-NON-EDITED-FIELDS.
        05   W3-NUMBER   PIC 99.
        05   W3-SQUARE   PIC 999.
        05   W3-CUBE     PIC 9999.
```

```
PROCEDURE DIVISION.
010-OPEN.
     OPEN OUTPUT PRINT-TABLE
     WRITE PRINTLINE FROM W1-COLUMN-HEADINGS
     MOVE SPACES TO PRINTLINE
     WRITE PRINTLINE
     MOVE 1 TO W3-NUMBER
     PERFORM 020-CALCULATE UNTIL (W3-NUMBER > 10)
     GO TO 030-CLOSE.
020-CALCULATE.
     MULTIPLY W3-NUMBER BY W3-NUMBER GIVING W3-SQUARE
     MULTIPLY W3-NUMBER BY W3-SQUARE GIVING W3-CUBE
     MOVE ZEROES TO W2-REPORT-LINE
     MOVE W3-NUMBER TO W2-NUMBER-OUT
     MOVE W3-SQUARE TO W2-SQUARE-OUT
     MOVE W3-CUBE TO W3-CUBE-OUT
     WRITE PRINTLINE FROM W2-REPORT-LINE
     ADD 1 TO W3-NUMBER.
030-CLOSE.
     CLOSE PRINT-TABLE
     STOP RUN.
```

6 SCREEN FORMATTING

In Micro Focus COBOL, there are several ways of formatting output to a screen. One way is to use PROCEDURE DIVISION statements. This is illustrated in the following programs.

```
* { This program clears the screen and displays messages   }
* { in the middle and bottom right hand parts of the screen }
* { Micro Focus COBOL version                               }
 IDENTIFICATION DIVISION.
 PROGRAM-ID.  TM71B.
 ENVIRONMENT DIVISION.
 SPECIAL-NAMES.
 CONSOLE IS CRT.
 DATA DIVISION.
 PROCEDURE DIVISION.
 010.
      DISPLAY SPACES
      DISPLAY "CENTRE" AT 1237
      DISPLAY "BOTTOM RIGHT" AT 2468
      STOP RUN.
```

CONSOLE IS CRT is declared in the SPECIAL-NAMES section of the ENVIRONMENT DIVISION. CRT stands for Cathode Ray Tube, the main component of the screen in a visual display unit.

The effect of DISPLAY SPACES is to clear the screen of anything displayed on it.

```
DISPLAY "CENTRE" AT 1237
```

displays the word 'CENTRE' on line 12 starting in column 37. AT 2468 represents line 24 column 68. AT 0101 would represent line 1 column 1 i.e. the top left hand corner of the screen.

The next program shows how the cursor may be positioned ready for input by the user – a data item is ACCEPTed AT the specified location on the screen. Notice that if COSOLE IS CRT is specified, the value of the first ACCEPT statement is not discarded – a declaration such as

```
01   W-JUNK   PIC X.
```

and the corresponding statement

```
ACCEPT W-JUNK
```

are not required.

```
* { This program ACCEPTs input at a screen location }
* { Micro Focus COBOL version                        }
 IDENTIFICATION DIVISION.
 PROGRAM-ID.  TM72B.
 ENVIRONMENT DIVISION.
 SPECIAL-NAMES.
 CONSOLE IS CRT.
 DATA DIVISION.
 WORKING-STORAGE SECTION.
 01   W-NAME   PIC X(20).
 PROCEDURE DIVISION.
 010.
     DISPLAY SPACES
     DISPLAY "Name?" AT 0620
     ACCEPT W-NAME AT 0628
     STOP RUN.
```

The cursor position is represented by a four-digit number.

```
01   W-CURSOR-POSITION.
     05   W-CURSOR-LINE     PIC 99.
     05   W-CURSOR-COLUMN   PIC 99.
```

W-CURSOR-LINE and W-CURSOR-COLUMN can be incremented to move the cursor in a systematic way, as shown in the following program.

```
* { This program displays a row of seats }
* { Micro Focus COBOL version            }
 IDENTIFICATION DIVISION.
 PROGRAM-ID.  TM73B.
 ENVIRONMENT DIVISION.
 SPECIAL-NAMES.
 CONSOLE IS CRT.
 DATA DIVISION.
 WORKING-STORAGE SECTION.
 01   W-SEAT   PIC XXX   VALUE "[ ]".
 01   W-CURSOR-POSITION.
     05   W-CURSOR-LINE       PIC 99.
     05   W-CURSOR-POSITION   PIC 99.
 PROCEDURE DIVISION.
 010.
     DISPLAY SPACES
     DISPLAY "MAGIC THEATRE COMPANY" AT 0529
     MOVE 8 TO W-CURSOR-LINE
     MOVE 27 TO W-CURSOR-COLUMN
     PERFORM 020-PRINT-ROW UNTIL (W-CURSOR-COLUMN > 53)
     GO TO 030.
 020-PRINT-ROW.
     DISPLAY W-SEAT AT W-CURSOR-POSITION
     ADD 3 TO W-CURSOR-COLUMN.
 030.
     STOP RUN.
```

Array elements can neither be ACCEPTed nor DISPLAYed AT specified locations on the screen. The array element could be MOVEd to another variable, then there should be no problem. For example, in the following program, the letters A to E are held in the array W-LETTER. A specified letter is DISPLAYed by

```
        MOVE W-LETTER (W-LETTER-NUMBER) TO W-SEAT-LETTER
        DISPLAY W-SEAT-LETTER AT W-CURSOR-POSITION


*  { This program displays a seating plan together with row       }
*  { letters.  It is a partial answer to question 2 exercise 7.1 }
*  { Micro Focus COBOL version                                    }
   IDENTIFICATION DIVISION.
   PROGRAM-ID.  TMA6B.
   ENVIRONMENT DIVISION.
   SPECIAL-NAMES.
   COSOLE IS CRT.
   DATA DIVISION.
   WORKING-STORAGE SECTION.
   01  W-SEAT    PIC X(3)   VALUE "[ ]".
   01  W-CURSOR-POSITION.
       05  W-CURSOR-LINE     PIC 99.
       05  W-CURSOR-COLUMN   PIC 99.
   01  W-SEAT-LETTERS   PIC X(5)   VALUE "ABCDE".
   01  FILLER REDEFINES W-SEAT-LETTERS.
       05  W-LETTER      PIC X   OCCURS 5 TIMES.
   01  W-LETTER-NUMBER   PIC 9.
   01  W-SEAT-LETTER     PIC X.
   PROCEDURE DIVISION.
   010-START.
       DISPLAY SPACES
       DISPLAY "MAGIC THEATRE COMPANY" AT 0529
       MOVE 08 TO W-CURSOR-LINE
       MOVE 1 TO W-LETTER-NUMBER
       PERFORM 020-PRINT-LINE UNTIL (W-CURSOR-LINE > 12)
       GO TO 040-STOP.
   020-PRINT-LINE.
       MOVE 25 TO W-CURSOR-COLUMN
       MOVE W-LETTER (W-LETTER-NUMBER) TO W-SEAT-LETTER
       DISPLAY W-SEAT-LETTER AT W-CURSOR-POSITION
       ADD 2 TO W-CURSOR-COLUMN
       PERFORM 030-PRINT-SEAT UNTIL (W-CURSOR-COLUMN > 51)
       ADD 1 TO W-CURSOR-LINE
       ADD 1 TO W-LETTER-NUMBER.
   030-PRINT-SEAT.
       DISPLAY W-SEAT AT W-CURSOR-POSITION
       ADD 3 TO W-CURSOR-COLUMN.
   040-STOP.
       STOP RUN.
```

7 MODULAR PROGRAMMING

The Micro Focus compiler outputs intermediate code to a file named programname
.INT. Programs are CALLed via their intermediate code filename. So, for example, if
program TMCREATE.CBL was compiled, TMCREATE.INT would be produced by
the compiler and TMCREATE.INT could be CALLed from another program.

```
* { This program passes control to other programs by CALLing }
* { them.  Micro Focus COBOL version                         }
 IDENTIFICATION DIVISION.
 PROGRAM-ID.  MENUB.
 ENVIRONMENT DIVISION.
 DATA DIVISION.
 WORKING-STORAGE SECTION.
 01  W-CHOICE  PIC X.
 01  W-DONE    PIC X(5).
 PROCEDURE DIVISION.
 010-CONTROL.
     MOVE SPACES TO W-DONE
     PERFORM 020-MENU UNTIL (W-DONE = "TRUE")
     GO TO 030-END.
 020-MENU.
     MOVE SPACES TO W-CHOICE
     DISPLAY "Menu: C(reate, P(rint, S(earch, E(xit: "
     ACCEPT W-CHOICE
     IF (W-CHOICE = "E" OR "e")
         MOVE "TRUE" TO W-DONE
     ELSE IF (W-CHOICE = "C" OR "c")
         CALL "CREATEB.INT"
     ELSE IF (W-CHOICE = "P" OR "p")
         CALL "PRINTB.INT"
     ELSE IF (W-CHOICE = "S" OR "s")
         CALL "SEARCHB.INT"
     ELSE
         DISPLAY W-CHOICE " NOT UNDERSTOOD".
 030-END.
     STOP RUN.


* { This program is CALLed by the menu program.  It displays }
* { a message on the screen and then returns control to the  }
* { menu program.  Micro Focus COBOL version                 }
 IDENTIFICATION DIVISION.
 PROGRAM-ID.  CREATEB.
 ENVIRONMENT DIVISION.
 DATA DIVISION.
 PROCEDURE DIVISION.
 010.
     DISPLAY "File CREATION program called".
 020.
     EXIT PROGRAM.
```

Notice that the empty USING list in the PROCEDURE DIVISION header is not
required, and that EXIT PROGRAM is the only statement in its paragraph.

Index